Mary Francis Cusack

The Life of Father Mathew

The People's Soggarth Aroon

Mary Francis Cusack

The Life of Father Mathew
The People's Soggarth Aroon

ISBN/EAN: 9783744660020

Printed in Europe, USA, Canada, Australia, Japan

Cover: Foto ©Lupo / pixelio.de

More available books at **www.hansebooks.com**

THE LIFE

OF

FATHER MATHEW,

The People's Soggarth Aroon.

BY

SISTER MARY FRANCIS CLARE,

AUTHOR OF THE "ILLUSTRATED HISTORY OF IRELAND," "ADVICE
TO IRISH GIRLS IN AMERICA," "HORNE-HURST RECTORY,"
"LIFE OF SAINT PATRICK," ETC., ETC.

NEW YORK:

D. & J. SADLIER & COMPANY,

31 BARCLAY STREET.

MONTREAL:—COR. NOTRE DAME & ST. FRANCIS XAVIER STS.

1872.

CONTENTS.

CHAPTER VIII.

CHAPTER IX.

CHAPTER X.

CHAPTER XI.

CHAPTER XII.

CHAPTER XIII.

CHAPTER XIV.

CONTENTS.   vii

CHAPTER XV.

THE

LIFE OF FATHER MATHEW.

CHAPTER I.

Father Mathew's birth-place — His early life — His affectionate
disposition — Love of his mother — His courage — Story of
the bad landlord — Father Mathew's vocation declared —
The zeal and mission of the Irish priest.

ATHER MATHEW was born in
the " old country," the land where
so many thousand good and true
priests have lived and died, and where not
a few have died the martyr's death and
won the martyr's crown. All have worked
in some way for God, but there are certain
individuals destined by Divine Providence
to a special mission, and if they are so hap-

py as to correspond with the favor granted to them, they leave the impress of their work on thousands, and the veneration of their name is from generation to generation.

Father Mathew was born at Thomastown, in the County Tipperary, on the 10th of October, 1790. It was a troublesome time, to be followed by one still more troubled. We all know what happened in '98, when poor Ireland made a hopeless effort to free herself from her chains. His father belonged to a family of high respectability, but he was a dependent upon the bounty of others. His mother is said to have been exceedingly beautiful, and evidently she was a very superior woman.

Theobald Mathew was her fourth son, and, it is said, her favorite. How little could she have anticipated his glorious career, or the honor in which his memory shall be held even to the end of time. We have said, to the end of time, but it would have been fitter to have said, throughout all eternity.

As the years roll on, and new members join the " Father Mathew Society ; " as now one husband and now another, one wife and now another, one son and now another, come proudly forward and join the grand phalanx of those who are free indeed, because they have ceased to be slaves to the most degrading of sins, the glory of our Apostle shall increase, his fame will extend more and more widely. Even now we may glance up at him near the great bright throne of God, and see the crowds of souls saved, saved from eternal woe by that great man's prayers, by that good man's labors. Pray for us, blessed father! You can still work for poor Ireland, and for the exiled Irish here below, by your prayers, as you once worked for us by your weary and incessant life of toil.

The little lad seems to have loved every one, and to have been loved by every one. The big heart which made him so ardently

desire the true prosperity of his country in
after life, already manifested itself in his
childhood. He was his mother's favorite,
certainly, but he was far from making this
an excuse or an apology for self-indulgence,
or tyranny over the younger children. His
greatest pleasure was to obtain for them
every gratification, every indulgence; his
greatest happiness was to provide them with
a " feast," the materials for which could
not be refused to his little loving caresses.

Thomastown, a lovely mansion, surrounded by a vast estate, was the property
of George Mathew, afterwards Baron, and
first Earl of Llandaff. When James Mathew's
family increased, he left Thomastown, which
he seems to have managed for his relatives,
and took a farm at Kathaloheen; but a
friendly intercourse was still kept up between the two families, and the Earl's
daughter, Lady Elizabeth, though many
years older than Theobald, never lost her
affection for him.

Yet with all his gentleness, or, rather, we should say, because of it, the boy was brave and full of courage, full of that grand courage of endurance which is often the most difficult as it is the least esteemed manifestation of this virtue. He could not, indeed, bear to see even a poor animal suffer, and how much more did he not feel for the sufferings of his fellow-creatures. He heard of the cruelties which a neighboring gentleman had exercised on the peasantry, and he heard, also, the strange stories of the friends or neighbors of the victims, who believed the unfortunate man was as fiendish in personal appearance as he had proved himself in action.

Theobald was determined to judge for himself, if possible, of the truth of these reports. He rose one morning early for this purpose, and without a thought of fear galloped across the country on his pony to the gentleman's demesne.

There he waited patiently for hours, but

2

the anticipated result did not occur, and
hunger compelled him to return home without a sight of the evil doer.

On another occasion, also, he proved his
physical powers by the fact of walking nearly forty miles in one day when only twelve
or thirteen years of age. He had been
placed at a good school in Kilkenny by
Lady Elizabeth Mathew, but when Easter
came the desire to see his parents, above all
to see his mother, proved too much for his
patience, and he set out on foot for home.
The welcome he received more than compensated his weariness, and the deeply affectionate nature of the man was shown by his
frequent references in after life to this little
episode, and the gratification with which
he spoke of his mother's fond welcome.

Theobald had nine brothers, and Mrs.
Mathew, with the characteristic piety of her
race, ardently desired that one of her sons
should be consecrated to the service of
God. How large a share her fervent

prayers may have had in the future career of her beloved boy we can never know in this world; but, one day, this and many other holy secrets will be rewarded.

One boy, George, had been, indeed, destined for the church, but he soon proved that he had no vocation. " Is it not unfortunate!" the good mother exclaimed one day. " Is it not unfortunate! I have nine sons, and not one of them to be a priest." But Theobald started from his seat, and exclaimed, with a voice full of emotion, " Mother don't be uneasy, I will be a priest!"

He had long been called the "Saint" of the family; he was now to prepare for that most holy office in and by which he was to sanctify his own soul, and the souls of thousands yet unborn.

On the 10th of September, 1807, Theobald Mathew abandoned the world and entered the College of Maynooth, that asylum of peace and sanctity from whence so many learned and gifted men have gone forth to sow the good seed of Faith throughout the world. What the Catholic Church has owed, still owes, and shall ever owe to the Irish *soggarth*, may not be told in this life, but the tale of faithful service shall as surely be told in the next, as the reward of faithful service shall be given.

It may, indeed, console the pride of those who are Catholics only in name, or at least but lukewarm followers of a crucified God, to fling a sneer at the " Irish soggarth," just because his manner, or his accent, differs a little from theirs ; but in heaven there will be only one manner, and one accent, one speech, and one language, and yet even there we shall find differences and distinctions, but these differences will be differences of merit, and the distinctions will be distinctions of reward, and the Irish priest with his thousands of faithful penitents shall hold his place gloriously, while those who once dared to despise him shall only see their error when it is too late to repair it.

Where would the English Catholics obtain the priests for their churches but for
the Irish, the faithful Celt, full of the zeal
of Divine love, who has renounced all
earthly pleasures to convert them, like a
second Patrick? And it is he who goes
across the wide Atlantic, goes east, goes
west, goes wherever there are souls to win
for God or keep safe for God, goes with
the message of peace to all men. Let him
be blessed. Let his hands be strengthened
and his heart be comforted. He asks only
one thing. He desires only one thing. Give
God your soul, keep it from the devil,
work for heaven, go there when you die.
Is it not this he asks of you? Is it for your
advantage, or for his? Give him generously all the help you can by word and deed,
for in giving a little to him you give an
abundance to yourself.

2*

1

CHAPTER II.

How Father Mathew came to join the Order of St. Francis of Assisi — His love of giving pleasure to others — Difference between the duties of a parish priest and a friar — Father Mathew in Kilkenny — His trouble there — How he was tried even by good people — How he bore a false accusation — He goes to Cork.

HE ways in which God guides souls are very wonderful; and we see these ways sometimes in a remarkable manner when He has a great work for any man in the future. Then the man is led, often by ways that seem strange and painful, to the end for which God designs him, and then even mistakes are overruled for the better accomplishment of the designs of Providence.

We see this overruling power in the early life of Father Mathew. My readers probably know that priests are known as

secular and religious. The secular priests
are under the control of a bishop, and are
occupied with the charge of souls in certain
parishes, to which, under ordinary circumstances, their ministrations are confined.

The religious Orders are governed by
their own Superiors, and are sent hither and
thither according to the work for which
they are best suited, so that the Church
wonderfully provides for the necessities of
her children. If the parish priest or curate
left his regular habitation, the people would
suffer grievously by his absence ; but there
are times and circumstances when the parish
priest needs more help, more assistance to
carry on his glorious work, and then he has
the good religious and the friar ready at
his call ; ready to give missions, to hear confession, or to preach on special occasions.

Now, if father Mathew had been a secular priest, he would have been obliged to
live always in the one place. He could not
have carried out the great and active work

for which God had destined him. We shall see how a mistake, or want of prudence, in his early life at Maynooth was, may we not say, the happy cause of his being a religious, of his entering the glorious Order of St. Francis, of that great Saint whom he resembled in so many ways.

It is a strict rule at Maynooth, and a very proper one, that no student should enter the room of another student under any circumstances. It is of course a still more strict prohibition against two or three meeting together, particularly for any kind of entertainment.

We all know how boys at school enjoy· the pleasure of a stolen feast, and boys who go to Maynooth have the same dispositions and inclinations as other boys, only they have a grander and nobler end in view in their collegiate course, and so they rarely yield to temptations to which others easily give way, and which in others would be very trifling faults.

We know that the young Theobald from
his early childhood delighted in giving
feasts to his brothers and sisters; probably
he did the same thing at school, and it is
more than probable that he did not think it
any harm to make the attempt at Maynooth.

But expulsion was the penalty for such a
proceeding. Young Theobald made the
attempt, and to prevent the public disgrace
of expulsion with which he was threatened
as a necessary consequence, he left the College in 1808.

But his fault, if fault this was, for he had
certainly no intention or idea of an overt
act of disobedience, led to the most happy
result. The young and thoughtful student
had been much struck by the demeanor of
two aged Franciscan Friars whom he had
seen in Kilkenny, and he at once determined
to seek admission into this Order. And now
I must say a few words about this Order,
and I may be pardoned for the digression,

because it is the Order to which the Apostle
of Ireland belonged, and I may be permitted
a little natural affection for it myself, since I
also am an unworthy member of the same
Order.

The Franciscan Order was founded by
St. Francis of Assisi in the year 1206. St.
Francis was the son of a wealthy Italian merchant, and he gave up all he possessed or
hoped to possess that he might live and die
poor like our dear Lord, who had not where
to lay His head. On one occasion it is re-
lated of the Saint that he went through a
town with his disciples to preach, but never
a word did he say from the time he entered
the town until he left it. His disciples were
not a little amazed ; all the more so, because
he said, " My brothers, have we not preached well to-day." " But, Father," they replied, " you never said a word." " It is
true, my brothers, but for all that we
preached." And then he explained to them
that the poverty of their dress preached

poverty, and the meekness of their manner preached humility, and the devotion of their appearance preached piety—and, in truth, it must have been in some such manner that the old friars in Kilkenny preached to young Theobald Mathew, for they said never a word, but for all that they obtained a new glory for their Order, and a disciple for St. Francis after his own heart.

Father Mathew was consecrated priest on Easter Sunday in the year 1814 by the Most Rev. Dr. Murray, the Archbishop of Dublin. His first sermon was delivered in the Parish Church of Kilfeade, County Tipperary, where he said Mass for the parish priest. His subject was the gospel of the day, which told how difficult it was for a rich man to enter the kingdom of Heaven.

A rich man was present; his name was Scully, he possessed much land and much wealth, and as the good, young priest truthfully explained that it was not the fact of possessing riches which kept people out of

Heaven, but the bad use of them, he flattered himself that he of course did not make a bad use of them.   He made a pleasant joke, at all events, for he thanked Father Mathew for trying to squeeze him through the eye of the Gospel needle, and as he was enormously stout, the joke told very well.

Father Mathew was now sent to the very friars at Kilkenny whose example had been the immediate cause of his vocation to their Order.   He now became quite famous as a preacher, and not alone as a preacher, but even as a director.   Young as he was, even the aged were not ashamed, but rather were anxious to come to him for counsel, not only in spiritual matters, but even in difficult temporal affairs.

Every one said there was " something angelic" about him ; and so there was, for his great heart was full of love to God, and thus it was indeed that he became like unto an angel.   His great work was in the Confessional, from which he was rarely absent, not only on holidays, and on the eves of great festivals, but on every day of the week and all day long.

Pardon me for saying a word about this weary duty of the good priest. How little people think of the pain and trouble attached to his sacred office! They complain if the priest cannot hear them at once, they complain if they are kept waiting a few minutes, they will not wait if they are detained a little from business or even from pleasure; but look at the priest, see how he is occupied hour after hour, day after day, night after night! Do you hear him complain, do you hear him say a word? Do you suppose that he does not feel pain and fatigue and weariness like other people? He suffers this for hours, day after day, week after week, and you complain of it if you have to suffer just a little now and then.

Father Mathew began also to be noticed as a preacher. His voice was shrill and weak and his manner was not very attractive, but

3

he was in earnest. He spoke to souls, and for God, with all his heart; and when men do that, all exterior hindrances become of little account.

But Father Mathew was to be prepared for his great and glorious work by a sore trial and humiliation. The priests of religious orders were not allowed to hear the Easter confessions of their penitents, for, as we know, it is a strict regulation of the Church that we should all go to confession and communion in our own parish church once a year.

Some persons, who were jealous of all the good done by the young friar, informed the Bishop that he had not kept this rule.

The Bishop did not wait to make further enquiries. Perhaps he thought his informant was a sufficient authority, and perhaps God allowed him to judge hastily for the greater merit of the good father.

One thing at least is certain; while Father Mathew sat in his box, and was surrounded by crowds, a messenger appeared in all haste,

and handed him a letter. He read it quietly and then rose from his seat, saying to
those around him, "Go to the other clergy-
men, for I have no longer authority to hear
your confessions." And then the noble, humble friar gently left the church.

How great the trial was, to one of his
sensitive, affectionate nature, none but God
might know! But God did know it, and
Father Mathew was not unfaithful to the
grace which God gave him in his hour of
trial. How different his conduct was from
that which we have unhappily seen even in
our own day and time! He heard but to
obey. He knew he was accused falsely ;
but had not his Master also been accused
falsely, and had He not taught his children
the example of silent submission as an act of
the most heroic virtue ?

If Father Mathew had rebelled against
his lawful superior, he might have had the
sympathy of a few ignorant or unfaithful
people, he might have attempted to justify

himself on the plea that he was not guilty of
the fault of which he was accused; but the
sympathy even of all the world would have
availed him but little even here, and it
would have availed him nothing in eternity.
The plea of not guilty, though perfectly just,
would not have been accepted at the Last
Great Day as an excuse for rebelling against
authority to which he was bound to submit
so long as that authority demanded nothing
that was sinful.

It often happens that such trials come to
those whom God has specially gifted for a
special work. They are a preparation for
the work, and a test of fitness for it. Those
who fail in the trial are generally consigned
to obscurity; if they conquer, by God's
grace, they enter on a long career of usefulness which will bring great glory to God,
great good to the Church, and great merit
to their own souls.

CHAPTER III.

ATHER MATHEW now removed
to Cork, where there were a few
members of his order in a convent
which had been founded by the famous
Franciscan friar, Father O'Leary. His superior was a Father Donovan, a priest scarcely
less famous among the people, though not so
well-known to the public. He had narrow-
ly escaped execution during the Irish revolution, and his thankfulness for his deliverance manifested itself in the very holy and
practical form of a special devotion to prepare condemned prisoners for execution.
With that delicate kindness which is in-

3*

separable from the highest sanctity, he cared
not only for their spiritual, but even for their
temporal necessities. Many and many a
joke went the rounds of Cork at the good
friar's expense, for he " lent " his clothes so
often to these poor fellows to die in, and
" borrowed " so often from his friends when
he was reduced to the direst poverty; a
poverty that was as real as the good St.
Francis could possibly have desired.

Though differing remarkably in manner
and appearance, he and Father Mathew were
soon the greatest friends. They had indeed
but the one object at heart, and each had
this object so much, so entirely at heart,
that they could not have any serious differences as to the way of carrying it out.

Father Mathew soon became as much
sought in the confessional in Cork as he
had been in Kilkenny ; but he did not now
keep himself to the one work. He began
to prepare, and then to execute certain
plans for the benefit of his penitents, and,

indeed, of all the poorer classes, who were the special objects of his tenderest care.

Schools were then scarcely heard of, and any attempt to give an education which should combine literature and industry was entirely unknown. But Father Mathew set an example which has since been followed by hundreds. He established schools at the " Little Friary," as the poor houses were called where the Franciscan Fathers lived, and soon some five hundred children reaped the benefit of his care.

Father Mathew's natural qualities were of no little service to him in his great work. He was, as we know, extremely affectionate and fond of young people ; he used the talent to win their hearts, not for himself, but for his God. He had a certain aptitude for business; he used this talent to work for his Maker's service. He had a naturally energetic character; he devoted every particle of his energy to the service of Heaven.

While other men with great talents were misusing their gifts by abusing them, he had employed his for the best and holiest ends. He required Divine grace to enable him to do this, for no amount of even natural gifts will enable us to persevere in good, or in doing good; but God never refuses us this grace, and the more we use it, the more is given to us to use.

The good priest rose every morning at four o'clock, and even earlier. We may be sure that no amount of natural inclination could enable a man to persevere in such an act of self-denial without any personal advantage, and few even could do it for temporal gain unless compelled by stern necessity.

A friend once inquired how it was that Father Mathew was able to continue the practice of early rising. Pointing to a cooper's work-shop in the immediate neighborhood, he replied, "If I were a cooper, and bound to Mr. T——, I should be up as early

so as to be at my work at the appointed
time, and thus become pleasing to Mr.
T——, my master. But I have a higher
motive, and I serve a better Master, and am
I to be less desirous of serving that Master
than I should be to satisfy Mr. T——?"

It is true, indeed, that a priest is bound
in an especial manner to the service of
God, but are we not all bound to that service also? In truth, if we only understood
our own interest, it is the service of all
others, and above all others, to which we
should devote ourselves. Our reward is
certain, our promotion sure. Our reward
will be eternal, our promotion will be forever, and forever. What fools we are to
neglect so glorious an opportunity! The
man who refuses to work for the Master
who gives the easiest labor and the largest
pay is considered a fool. What should we
say of the man who neglects that eternal
remuneration, and that eternal reward,
which he may so easily obtain, and at so

very small a sacrifice of time or inclination?

But the devil will tempt them? Certainly he will. It is his business—his evil wicked business; but, my friends, it is our business to resist the devil. A soldier going into battle might as well say "The enemy will attack me." Of course he will. What does a man go into battle for except to fight and win the victory, and if he does not care for the cause in which he is fighting, he does not deserve the honor and the glory of success, or the credit given to those who fall when doing their bravest or their best.

We are all fighting with the devil for heaven, or we ought to be. The place is worth fighting for, and only those who fight well and bravely shall win the day. And this fight is not like human conflicts, in which success is uncertain, or depending on many causes over which the poor soldier, however well he may serve, has no control.

A man who goes out to fight for his country, or his liberty, or even his religion, may never get the reward of his valor in this world at least; but a man who goes out to fight for heaven—if he is only in earnest, if he only uses the means that are offered to him, that are provided for him, can never fail, can never lose the victory.

I pray you, my friends, to think a little about this. It is a grand thing to fight for one's country, for one's liberty, for freedom for old Ireland; but it is a still grander thing to fight for heaven. Political freedom can only serve us just so long as we live in this world. We can only serve our earthly country just so long as we are in the flesh. But think of eternal freedom, of that freedom which shall last for more years than there are drops of water in the ocean, stars in the sky, or sands on the sea-shore. Yes! if you could count the stars, and the sands, and the drops of water, and then when you had counted them, multiply them by millions and millions, you could not have even reckoned up one-half the years of eternity, for eternity shall never end.

Think how terrible it would be to lose your freedom for all these ages! Think how terrible, how dreadful it would be to be chained in a pit of fire and darkness, to be tortured for all these ages! Oh! that would be slavery, that would be the loss of freedom, to which all human slavery, all human loss of liberty would be but as if you imprisoned a sunbeam for a second.

Suppose that you imprisoned a bird for just a minute, and then let it free, what would result? It would feel pain at its captivity for that second, but when you let it free, it would soar away through the blue sky singing, and all thought of its pain would be gone. Such are the effects of earthly captivity, of loss of temporal liberty, when compared with eternal freedom.

But if you placed that poor imprisoned bird in a fiery furnace and could keep it there, still living, still suffering, year after year—oh! how terrible its fate would be.

My friends, this is what the devil wishes to do with us. He has lost his own liberty, his own freedom; he is forever in torment, wherever he may be, and his own evil wicked desire is to put us in torment also, to deprive us of our liberty, to make us as wretched as himself, as despairing as he is himself.

In order to accomplish this purpose he tempts us. He is wise enough, for he is still a spirit, though fallen. He has the knowledge of the angel, which he once was, with the craft and cunningness of the devil, which he now is. He knows very well that if he came to us openly and said, " Will you go to hell?" that we would refuse to go, so he is obliged to entice us there, to persuade us to go, fancying all the time, that we are pleasing ourselves. How miserable, how wretchedly miserable will be our state, when we come to see that we were pleasing the

4

devil all the time that we thought we were enjoying our liberty !

I have said already that when God intends any soul to do a great work for his glory, He generally allows that soul to be sorely tried. There may be two reasons for this, first, because trials prove our virtue; we cannot tell whether a man is a brave soldier or not, until he has seen fight. Second, because people who have been tempted themselves know best how to help others to resist temptations, even as a man who has seen long service in the wars is better fitted to lead on an army to fight than a raw recruit.

Father Mathew was to be the Apostle of Temperance. The devil probably knew this, for the fallen spirits know many things of which we are ignorant, or can at least make better guesses about the future, and so the devil, knowing all the good that might be done by him, and all the souls that might be saved from eternal misery, deter-

mined to try what he could do to hinder
Father Mathew from his great work by
tempting him to the very vice from which
he was to save thousands.

The difference between the saints and ourselves is clearly seen here. We are tempted and the saints are tempted, but the
saints resist temptation generously, they
are the true freemen, and we yield to it, and
are miserable slaves.

Father Donovan died about the year 1820.
We know how Father Mathew loved him,
and what a truly affectionate heart the good
priest had. He would not have been a true
Irishman if he had not mourned for his friend.
There is no virtue in hardheartedness. I
thank God, the worst enemies of old Ireland
have never charged us with that. There is
no religion in being indifferent to others;
people who do not care for others are seldom
good Christians; they are generally indifferent to God if they are indifferent to their
neighbors. But it was not so with our
glorious *soggarth.*

He wept for his old friend, who was to him at once as a superior and a father. Perhaps he yielded a little too much to grief, we do not know, we cannot tell; God alone knows every heart, and the failings of every heart He alone can judge.

One thing is certain that good Father Mathew gave way to grief, even to some degree of despondency; that he refused to visit his friends, who kindly tried to console him in his sorrow. But they did what they could for him according to their ideas of friendship, and one person sent him some spirits, which was then, as alas! by too many now, considered a patent remedy in such cases.

But Father Mathew did not care for spirits, and it lay in the cupboard untouched. Evening came, the room was dark and gloomy, poor Father Mathew was weary from his long day's work, he missed more than ever the gentle voice and pleasant word of his dear old Father Donovan,

he sat down by his lonely fire, and as it
became darker and darker, and his poor
loving heart became more and more sad, he
heard a voice, it was the voice of the devil,
but the devil knows very well how to dis-
guise himself.

" Father Mathew," he said, "that liquor
in the cupboard is delicious. You have not
tasted it. Why don't you try it?"

Father Mathew, absorbed in his sorrow,
did not seem to notice the strange voice at
first, and only said quietly,

" Tea is much better."

But the enemy was not to be stopped so
easily, and he spoke again—

" But you did not taste the liquor; it is
delicious; only try it."

Yes! that was just all he wanted, "only
try it," " only have a taste," "just one drop to
keep up your spirit." Oh, my friends! how
many thousands and thousands has the devil
got to hell by tempting them, not indeed
openly, as he did Father Mathew, but in

4*

secret in their hearts, or by the voice of a friend—" Why not try it? Only taste a drop," and one taste led on to another, and "one drop" to another, until the poor soul was dragged down to hell, where he must thirst and thirst forever, without one drop, of water to satisfy his terrible and never-ceasing cry.

Father Mathew knew it was the devil now, but he was a holy man, and he resisted temptation. He did not try to answer or to argue with the fiend, but he took refuge in flight.

He seized his hat and ran to the parish priest at once, a good old man, and told him all. This priest was Father Collins, then in his seventieth year. He assured the young friar that it was the devil, of which indeed there could be no doubt, and told him he had done well to resist the temptation. But our good *soggarth* was not satisfied with merely resisting temptation, he took care also to keep it from him. He took care to avoid further occasions of danger.

Next morning, he sent the bottle of spirits to a friend, and thus ended the temptation, and thus was the glorious victory won. And in this also, we have another great lesson.

It is the abuse of intoxicating drinks which is so dangerous, and not the proper use of them. Those who can use them in moderation, may do so; but when there is the least danger, the only safety is in flight from all occasions of temptation, and in TOTAL ABSTINENCE.

Another trouble came soon after. How happy it was that the good father wâs so well prepared to meet it! He had taken a young brother to live with him, soon after the death of Father Donovan. The boy repaid his brother's love, by the kindest, tenderest affection; but like many another youth, he had a taste for roaming, and this was so irresistible, that Father Mathew was obliged to allow him to indulge it.

An elder brother was trading in Africa,
and he took the boy with him. Here he
found an early grave, and died of sun-stroke
after a few hours' illness. This was a terrible blow to the priest. He looked, day
after day, for the boy's return, whom he
loved almost as a mother. Day after day,
when the lad was with him, he had hidden
himself behind a door about the time when
he expected Father Mathew to return from
his duties in the schools, or from visiting
the poor, and day after day he repeated the
same loving trick, by springing out on him,
to give and receive a surprise, and a fond
caress.

To the boy the freshness of youth made
the trick always new. The fondness of love
made it always dear to the priest. He
hoped, day after day, as he came home, for
the same pleasant surprise; but the arms
which had wound round him so often and
so fondly were already mouldering in dust.

Our good Father had a severe struggle

for resignation, but grace prevailed over nature. It is true, indeed, that for a long
time he could not speak of the lad without
tears; but they were tears of resignation,
and such tears will only enhance the future
glory of him by whom they were shed.

Like all those who are gifted with unusual intellect, and with warm affections, he
felt any word or act of injury or unkindness more keenly than others, and, perhaps, as such persons do generally, far more
severely than those who inflict such pain
can ever be aware—at least, one might hope
so, for there is much unnecessary pain
given to others by thoughtless and selfish
natures.

But the priest and the friar triumphed
over the man, or rather the grace of God
prevailed over natural inclinations and natural imperfections. We too often hear people
excuse themselves for their faults on the
plea that " they cannot help them," a miserable excuse even from a merely human

point of view, for a man thereby declares
himself to be a weak, wretched creature,
and is unworthy of the honor of manhood.

But it is worse than miserable as regards
his soul, his immortal being. It is true, indeed, that of ourselves we can do no good
thing, no act which can merit the favor of
God; but it is also true that God never refuses His grace to those who ask for it
humbly and sincerely; therefore, if we fail,
we have only ourselves to blame, and the
loss is surely ours.

Father Mathew used to say, "A pint of
oil is better than a hogshead of vinegar;"
and what he preached to others, he prac-
ticed himself. He used to say that when he
was tempted to anger, or resentment, he
struggled hard with the bitterness of the
moment, "and then the rest was easy."

There is an old Irish proverb which says
that the "first step is the most difficult,"
and like many a wise saying of the old
times there is much truth in these words.

They are certainly true in all encounters
with the enemy of our souls. If we resist
at once, by God's grace, we are sure to
gain the victory; but if we hesitate and
have a talk with the devil before we make
up our minds to fight, we are putting ourselves in his power, and we are losing some
of the grace so necessary for us in order to
gain the victory.

Father Mathew had great use for his
"pint of oil" on one special occasion; indeed, I am not sure that he would not have
required several pints, for the circumstances
were very trying.

A lady (Why will women do mischief
with their tongues?) thought it her "duty"
(When will some women learn that making
mischief is never a duty?) to tell Father
Mathew that another priest had spoken
very unkindly of him at a dinner party before a great number of people. It is not
very pleasant to hear that we have been
spoken evil of; in fact, one-half the quarrels

in the world arise from the repetition of
such conversations; but it is above all hard
when the person who speaks evil of us is
just the very person who ought not to
do it.

We may be tolerably sure that the story
did not lose in the carriage, for those who
are wicked enough to carry stories, are
generally wicked enough to exaggerate
what they hear, and make the very worst
of it. The story was told, but the lady was
not a little amazed at the reply. Father
Mathew had used his pint of oil so often
that he was now quite master of himself; he
had taken the first step long ago, he had
corresponded generously with God's grace,
and God was ready to help him in his time
of need.

"My dear madam," he said, "I am very
sorry, indeed, that my actions have not the
approbation of this clergyman, for he is a
truly good man, and one whose good opinion I value highly, and I only hope that I

may merit it in future more than I have
hitherto done."

The lady was not too well pleased,
for her mission of mischief had failed, and
her vexation with Father Mathew was a
proof, if proof were needed, that her object
was certainly not his good, or the good of
religion.

Some time after, the same priest got a
fever while attending the sick. He died of
it, but the very first clergyman who came
to him was Father Mathew, and he was also
the most watchful attendant at his sick-bed.
I think we may be a little proud of our noble
Irish *soggarth;* but, perhaps, it would be
better if we prayed for grace to imitate his
holy example.

5

CHAPTER IV.

ATHER MATHEW now began to be famous as a preacher. For many years his ministrations were principally confined to the poor; and the good and true follower of St. Francis, who always loved the poor so dearly, was well contented that it should be so. But after a time, first one gentleman came, and then another, and then a few more, to hear what this man had to say, in whose praises the "old women" were so eloquent. They were very much astonished and edified. The holy friar used no words of human

(50)

eloquence, neither was he what the world calls a clever preacher. He was too simple to use flowers of rhetoric, but he was also too loving not to use every word of tenderness that could be used to win poor sinners to their God.

His sermons on the Passion, and especially those which he preached on Good Friday, made strong men sob and cry. He told them of all that had been suffered for their sins, as one would do who loved Jesus so much that he could scarcely bring himself to tell of all his bitter pains, yet as one who loved souls so much that he desired to give them all the help he could, to enable them to reap the fruit of the sufferings of their God.

He also preached many charity sermons, a task for which he was especially fitted, since his own life was one continued act of charity. An extract from one of the sermons will show his style, and it will also show how common charity was amongst

the lower classes in Ireland, as it is, thank
God, in the present day :

" If I were to pause to enumerate but the
hundredth-part of the many generous deeds
of mercy performed by the poorest of the
poor, of which I, myself, have been witness,
I would occupy the whole of the time which
this discourse should last.   Permit me,
however, to state one simple case of facts :—
A poor woman found in the streets a male
infant, which she brought to me, and asked
imploringly, what she was to do with it.
Influenced, unhappily, by cold caution, I
advised her to give it to the Poor-Law
guardians.   It was then evening.   On the
ensuing morning early, I found this poor
woman at my door; she was a poor water-
carrier; she cried bitterly, and said: ' I
have not slept one wink all night for part-
ing with that child which God had put in
my way, and if you will give me leave, I
will take him back again.'   I was filled
with confusion at the pious tenderness of

this poor creature, and I went with her
to the parish nurse, for the infant, which
she brought to her home with joy, ex-
claiming, in the very words of the proph-
et — 'Poor child, though thy mother has
forgotten thee, I will not forget thee.' Eight
years have elapsed since she brought to her
humble home that exposed infant, and she is
now blind from the constant exposure to
wet and cold, and ten times a day may be
seen that poor water-carrier, passing with
her heavy load, led by this little foundling-
boy. Oh, merciful Jesus! I would gladly
sacrifice the wealth and power of this wide
world, to secure to myself the glorious
welcome that awaits this poor blind water-
carrier, on the great accounting-day. Oh!
what, compared to charity like this, the
ermined robe, the ivory sceptre, the golden
throne, the jewelled diadem."

His work was to preach for the poor, as
he believed that when he preached for them,
he benefitted the rich. Certainly there are

5*

not two ways of going to heaven, neither will there be separate places there for the rich and for the poor, and while distinctions of rank should be respected here, because they are a part of God's providential ar-⁕rangement for time, we should never forget, whether we are rich or poor, whether our earthly rank is high or lowly, that our rank in eternity will depend *solely* upon our merit, upon our faithful correspondence with God's grace in this world.

Father Mathew commenced the great work of his life on the 10th of April, 1838. He had long seen and mourned over the misery caused in his native land by the demon Drink, a foul and filthy devil, a tyrannical and a wretched task-master. Talk of the slavery of the African, or the cruelties once exercised by the English enemy, why, it is but as a pin point, as the prick of a needle compared with the deadly, deadly agony and anguish and pain inflicted by the demon Drink.

At worst the foreign enemy could but en-
slave the poor body; the demon Drink en-
slaves both body and soul. But could the
former oppress the unhappy Celt in this
world, at the moment of death his power
would cease forever; but the demon Drink
could torture ages, and did torture and will
torture his victims to eternal ages.

At worst the cruel invader could but
drive a man from his earthly home, and
send him forth to wander a homeless pilgrim
for his life-time; but if he looked for a city
to come, for a home from which no tyranny
could eject him, he need care but little for
the trials of this life. But the demon Drink
would drive him out, not only from his
home in this world but also from his home
in the next. He would make his earthly
home the scene of misery, of crime, of
hatred, of poverty, of pain of body and soul,
but only, only, that he might inflict miseries
a thousand and a thousand times more hor-
rible in the life to come.

The cruelest landlord that ever ejected a tenant is mild and merciful compared with the demon, Drink. He drives his victims from the God-lit city, from the land of peace, from the Paradise of delight, from the Father's house where the faithful poor shall be rewarded eternally for all their temporal sufferings. He blears and blinds the eyes of his victims with the tears of maudlin sentimentality, and those tears, unless repented of in time, are not the tears which God shall wipe away with His own hand in the heavenly Jerusalem.

It was no wonder that Father Mathew desired to do something for his country, for he loved his country dearly; it was no wonder that he desired to save his people from the very worst of tyrannies, for he knew well the injury which the tyrant could do.

Mr. Martin, a member of the Society of Friends, had long urged Father Mathew to commence a temperance movement. But

Father Mathew knew very well what great difficulties there would be in the way of such an undertaking, and he probably foresaw that if he did commence it, he should give up his whole time, and even his life to it.

He acted with the prudence of true sanctity. We see that where there was the least danger of temptation, he did not hesitate for so much as a second ; in such cases delay is not only dangerous, but sometimes fatal; but it was quite another matter for him to take a work of great importance in hand, and he should first be quite sure that it was God's will and not his own.

After very much prayer and thought he determined at last to act. He sent for his friend William Martin, who deserved the epithet "honest" as well, and as truly, as the honest John Martin of our own day and time. The "friend" was overjoyed. He had obtained his heart's desire; all he needed now was to see the work commenced, and ·he had not long to wait.

Father Mathew appointed the evening of Tuesday, April 10, 1838, his school-house for the place, and seven o'clock in the evening for the time of meeting.

Father Mathew took the chair ; there were not many persons present; no one could have anticipated the glorious end which was to crown the work even in one short year. But as he said then in his first speech in the great Temperance cause, "if only one poor soul could be rescued from destruction, it would be giving glory to God, and well worth all the trouble."

Certainly, Father Mathew was right. We would think a great deal of any man who saved even one fellow-creature from a painful death, and if we were ourselves the person saved, our gratitude would have no bounds; but it was not a question of saving bodies alone, but of saving souls, and let us think what the loss of our souls would be, and let us think each for ourselves how we should love and revere those who help us to save *our souls.*

When Father Mathew had finished speak-
ing, he said, "Here goes in the name of God!"
and signed his name first of all in the grand
roll of Temperance heroes, of the brave men
and the true men who have saved their
own souls and the souls of others by taking
the Temperance Pledge. He signed his
name thus—"Rev. Theobald Mathew, C. C.,
Cove Street, No. 1."

My friends, that was truly "a great day
for Ireland," for Ireland, for England, for
America; for the example thus set has been
followed by millions, and, please God, will
be followed by millions and millions more.

"Here goes in the name of God!" Ah!
my dear friends, if you are one of those
whose very salvation, whose temporal
prosperity even depends upon doing like-
wise, I beg of you not to lose a moment. I
know my American friends love the poor
nun of Kenmare, as you fondly call me;
if you want to please me, if you want to
make me proud of you, go, go, in the name

of the good God ; don't wait to have a talk with the evil spirit, but go this minute to the priest, and take the pledge, and if it is impossible for you to go at once, kneel and promise God, in the name of the Father, and of the Son, and of the Holy Ghost, that you will take it the very first moment you can.

Go, in the name of God, and enroll your name in the Temperance Society of your own parish; be brave, be generous, save your poor soul, and disappoint the devil ; and when you and I, through God's mercy, meet at His great judgment-seat, be assured that you will not regret having followed my advice. Oh, my friends ! willingly would I give my life, over and over again, if I could persuade you to save your poor souls, and to be worthy of your glorious country. I pray you do not let old Ireland be taunted any longer for the faults of her unworthy sons.   Surely if the vice of drunkenness was unknown throughout Ireland, then Ireland would soon be "great, and glorious, and free;" if her sons would free themselves from the degrading chains of the demon Drink—no stranger could hold them long in captivity.

The public were now invited to attend Father Mathew's meetings, and as his school-room could not contain the numbers who flocked to hear him, and to take the pledge, he obtained the use of the Horse-Bazaar, a large open place where as many as 4,000 persons could easily assemble.

6

CHAPTER V.

How thousands came to take the pledge — Some account of Mr. Martin's style of address — He astonishes American tourists — The way in which Father Mathew gave the pledge — His great charity to the poor gets him into difficulties — A description of his room — How he practices poverty.

HE rapidity with which the members increased, may be judged from the fact, that in three months from the day on which Father Mathew said, " Here goes in the name of God," 25,000 people had signed his book; in five months, 13,000 more were enrolled, and at the close of the year 1838, there were 156,000. Many influential gentlemen now came forward, both to support the movement and to address the people at the meetings, which were held at least twice a week.

The good old "friend," now in his sixty-eighth year, was the happiest and busiest of men, and prided himself not a little on being the "grandfather of the cause."

It was indeed a work, it *is* a work in which every one bearing the Christian name should join, for its object is the salvation of souls, and the material benefit of the human race.

Mr. Maguire tells an admirable story of two American gentlemen, who went to hear William Martin speak on his favorite subject. He did not confine himself to the elegancies of language, for he was very much in earnest, as all men are, as all men must be, who have a great work in hand. He says:

" The writer well remembers the amazement depicted on the countenances of two American friends, whom Father Mathew had brought with him to a *'soirée,'* while listening to a speech from William. He was in majestic force this night, and seemed evidently determined to afford his transatlantic brethren a lively idea of how things

were done in Ireland. He revelled in comic
pictures and droll incidents, and he wound
up with his favorite queries, which clinched
the argument, and left his imaginary oppo-
nent trampled beneath his sturdy feet.
Imagine this broad - shouldered, vigorous
old man of seventy, roaring out the following questions and answers, his voice swell-
ing in volume, and his vehemence culmina-
ting to a force quite prodigious at the final
and crushing assertion: 'What does the
race-horse drink?—Water! What does the
lion drink?— Water!! What does the
elephant drink?—Water!!! It is good for
man, beast, and bird!!!!' As he shouted
out the last word, which he usually pro-
nounced as if it were spelt with a ' u ' instead
of an ' i,' he was carried away by his energy and literally roared and stamped, the
American friends looking on in indescribable
amazement, perhaps either dreading apoplexy for the impassioned orator, or the
sudden giving way of the floor, which, no

doubt, William sorely tried. Father Mathew thoroughly relished his friend William's exhibitions of 'earnestness and sincerity,' as he rather mildly termed these grand outbursts."

The following, which was accurately reported at the time—it was spoken in 1843 —will afford a valuable specimen of William Martin's gentler breathings.

"'Well, my friends, how things are changed! thanks to your good President. I remember the time, when I was the scoff and scorn of all Cork.' Here an old lady, from the fruit and vegetable market, with a deep lace frill to her snowy cap, which was ornamented with a broad ribbon of the most brilliant hue, remarked in a most consolatory tone—' Don't mind what they did, Mr. Martin, darling—'tis you had the sense, and they had not. God bless you! you knew what was good for poor craytures, and 'tis finely you are this blessed night, sure enough.' When the good-humored laughter which this sally provoked had

6*

subsided, the speaker continued his address ''Tis a great change for the better. But I knew it would be. When that meeting was held on the 10th of April, 1838, and your respected President undertook the task, I felt as if a load was taken off my shoulders, and put upon Theobald Mathew's.' Mr. Martin, finding his audience to be in the most amiable mood, thus pleasantly relaxed :—

" ' I will just tell you an anecdote, to show you how foolish a poor fellow may become when he has a little drop in. There was a man, named Turner, who thought that he should go to the public house and take a pint of ale ; he had two-and-sixpence in his pocket, besides the price of two pints. Well, John Turner went in and called for one pint, and then he called for another, and at last poor John Turner fell asleep. Now there were some 'purty boys' in the tap-room at the time, and they got a cork and burned it over the candle, and smeared poor John's face, until he became like a black. Well, one said that he ought to cut off one of John's whiskers; and when that one was off they did not think it was fair but to cut off the other, until John Turner was clipped as bare as a fighting-cock. 'Let us look at his pockets,' said they; and they looked in, and saw two-and-sixpence, and they took it out. After that they got a looking-glass and put it opposite to him, and then they shook him to waken him.

"' John opened his eyes, and rubbed them, and took a peep in the glass. 'Oh, dear! Is this me?' said John. 'No, it can't; it must be some other man. I was a fair man, and I had whiskers on me—and this fellow is black, and has not a hair on his face. Oh, dear! oh, dear!' said poor John. 'Who am I at all? Well, if it is true,' said John, 'I'll soon find out, for I had two-and-sixpence in my pocket; and if I have n't it, I can't be John Turner.' He put his hand in his pocket, and there was no two-and-sixpence to be found—so he said that he can't be

John Turner. He then thought, if any one should know it, it should be his wife; so he rolled and staggered to the door, and he rapped, and he says—'Is it here one John Turner lives?' 'It is,' says his wife, who opened the door. 'Am I John Turner, look at me and tell me, am I John Turner?' 'You are not John,' says the wife. 'John had a nice fair face, and had fine whiskers—and you have none; and John, oh! my John used to walk steadily and hold himself up like a man; but you are staggering about like a drunken fool, and you are nearly doubled up.' 'Oh, dear! oh, dear! then, who am I?' said John Turner. 'No matter who you are,' said the wife, 'you are in want of a lodging, and you must be taken in.' So she let him in, and I suppose when he awoke in the morning he found out that he was poor John Turner himself. It is said there is nourishment in strong drink; but I say it is in the eating, that the nourishment is to be found, When I eat, I find, as the lady said who took the pot of wine, that it is doing me good down to my very toes. Here I am in my seventy-second year, and I am strong and healthy without their nourishment. Oh! take the pure bubbling stream—

> ' Drink from the bubbling fountain free,
> 'T was Samson's drink, 't is good for thee.' "

There were 200,000 on the roll of the Society, July, 1839 — this multitude of free men ; for free men they may be truly called, since they were no longer slaves to a degrading vice which makes man contemptible, not only in the sight of God and His Holy Angels, but even before his fellow-creatures.

Those 200,000 were, of course, probably Cork men, but a good number were from Kerry and Clare, from Waterford and from Limerick, and even from distant Galway. People had begun to talk of the great work. People had begun to help in the great work.   The newspapers, fearful engines for good or bad—I thank God, in Ireland, at least, the good predominates—had begun to report Father Mathew's doings.

His fame was soon to go out to the ends of the earth, and certainly it had gone from one end of Ireland to another, had crossed the channel and astonished the slow-going Saxons.

To see Father Mathew; to take the pledge from him ; to be touched by him, and blessed by him ; this was sufficient reward for the longest and most painful journey. But never did Father Mathew send the poor pilgrim from his door, without having first fed and comforted him, and, where necessary, provided for his safe and easy return.   A seat in a public car, and a trifle in his pocket, enabled the poor traveler from a distance, often of fifty miles, sometimes of a h undred miles, to return happy and joyful to his home.   Thus, through the accounts given by the early pilgrims, of the good man, who had heard their story, who had sympathized with them, who had blessed them and prayed for them, who had treated them as a father and a benefactor, was the fame of Father Mathew spread abroad, even more effectually than through the columns of the public press.

The expense entailed on Father Mathew by what may be described as the pilgrimage to Cork, the Mecca of Temperance, was considerable; and before he ever sold a single medal, he was involved in debt, to the amount of £1,500, notwithstanding the numerous offerings which he continued to receive as a priest. His resources were not increased, but his expenditure, even thus early in the movement, was so, to a very great extent.

The lower apartment or parlor of his house, which was on a level with the street, was converted into a reception-room for those who came to take the pledge; and there was the book in which the names were

enrolled, and here the pledge was administered.   It was in this celebrated apartment
that scenes such as the following, might be
daily witnessed.   At all hours of the day
and evening, even to ten or eleven o'clock
at night, batches of ten, twenty or thirty
might be enrolled.   Some were sober and
penitent; others smelling strongly of their
recent potations, and ashamed to commit
themselves by uttering a word; others more
boisterous and rude, their poor wives and
mothers endeavoring to soothe and keep
them under control.   One of this class,—a
big brawny fellow, with rough voice, blood-
shot eyes and tattered clothes,—would roar
out, " I won't take the pledge, I'll be —— if
I do!   Is it me?   What occasion have I
for it?   I won't demane myself by taking it!
.Let me go, woman!   I tell you leave me
go !" "Oh, Patsy darling, don't expose yourself; you know I am for your good.   And
what would his reverence say to you, if he
heard you?   Do, alana, be quiet, and wait for

the holy priest." "Well, hould off of me at
any ratc. Can't I take care of myself?
Can't I do as I like? Who 'ill dare say I
can't?" "Oh, Patsy, Patsy darling! Is it indeed Patsy darling?" "Let me go, woman!"
and, bursting away from the trembling
hands of the poor creature who struggled
to hold the drunken fool, Patsy would make
a wild dash to the door, amid muttered
expressions of sympathy, such as, " God help
you, honest woman! 'Tis you are to be
pitied with that quare man." "Yes," another
would remark, "an' a fine man he is, and a
decent man, too; if he'd only be sober." But
just as Patsy was about effecting his escape,
and swearing that he would never be the
one of his name to demean himself, by taking their dirty pledge, he was certain to be
arrested by Father Mathew himself, who, at
a glance, knew the nature of the case.
Catching Patsy with a grasp stronger than
that from which he had escaped, Father
Mathew would say in a cheerful voice to

7

Patsy, as if that gentleman had come of his own free will, to implore the pledge at his hands:

" Welcome! welcome! my dear; delighted to see you! Glad you are come to me. You're doing a good day's work, for yourself and your family. You will have God's blessing on your head. Poverty is no crime, my dear child; it is sin alone that lowers us in the sight of God. Kneel down, my dear, (a strong pressure on Patsy's shoulder, under which, Patsy reluctantly sinks on his knees,) and repeat the words of the pledge, after me, and then I will mark you with the sign of the cross, and pray God to keep you from temptation." What could poor Patsy do, but yield, as that majestic hand rested affectionately on his tangled locks? And so Patsy's name was added to the long muster-roll of the pledged.

The good man had only one room besides the room where he slept; being a friar of the Order of St. Francis, he was especially bound to exercise the virtue of holy poverty, which is the great characteristic of that order, just as learning and devotion to the science of theology is the great object of the Dominicans or friar preachers.

His room was poor as poor could be; no carpet on the floor. What, indeed, would have been the use of it, if he had had one there, for it would have been worn away in two or three days from the constant trampling of heavy feet. But he had two framed pictures on his wall; one was a good engraving of the Holy Family, the other was done in needle work and represented the profession of St. Clare of Assisi, the first female disciple of St. Francis, and the founder of the Order of Poor Clares, which is, also, sometimes called the second Order of St. Francis.

CHAPTER VI.

How Father Mathew worked for God — His visit to Limerick — He is surrounded by thousands — His visit to May-nooth — Description of this visit by a student — He is said to have worked miracles — Some remarks on true and false miracles.

ATHER MATHEW still continu-ed his unceasing labors in Cork. His efforts, great as they were in the Temperance cause, were only an addi-tion to the many works with which he had previously burdened himself. But the time was soon to come when his whole life was to be given to the one object, when he was never to cease from his work of mercy un-til he went to find eternal mercy from the God whom he served so long and so faith-fully.

The city of Limerick was the first scene

of his missionary labors. He had been invited to visit that town by his venerable friend, the Right Rev. Dr. Ryan, a man simple and homely in manner, but of solid good sense, and true Christian piety. Father Mathew the more readily yielded to the invitation, as his doing so afforded him the opportunity of visiting his sister, Mrs. Dunbar, to whom he was tenderly attached, and to whom he had always stood more in the relation of a parent than a brother. The announcement of his intended visit—of the coming of the Apostle of Temperance—produced the most extraordinary effects, as it was borne from village to village, from town to town, from county to county, along the banks of the noble Shannon, and far away into the wilds of distant Connemara. Father Mathew, of whom mothers told their children, and of whom the old by the fireside spoke, his reverence was coming to Limerick! The first week in December, 1839, was a memorable time in that fine city.

7*

Even on the day before he was expected to
arrive, the principal roads were black with
groups of people from all parts of the county, from the adjoining counties, and from
the Province of Connaught.

During the next day the streets of Limerick were choked with dense masses—with
a multitude which it was impossible to
count, and whose numbers were guessed at,
as being something fabulous. It was an inva-
sion, a taking of the town by storm. The
necessaries of life rose to famine-prices. For
who could have anticipated such a mighty
rush? and where were food and drink to
be found by those myriad mouths? What
the authorities, the bishop and his clergy,
and the good citizens could do, to relieve
the necessities, and minister to the wants
of the strangers, they generously did. The
public rooms were laid open for their shelter
at night; for were the town ten times its
size, it could scarcely have afforded ordinary sleeping accommodation for those who

now stood in need of it. Father Mathew's
reception was an ovation such as few men
have ever received; indeed, still fewer had
ever excited in a people the same blended
feelings of love, and reverence, and enthusiasm. ˙

Though with a serious and solemn purpose in their minds, the people rushed
towards him as if possessed by a frenzy.
They struggled and fought their way
through living masses, through every ob-
stacle, until they found themselves in his
presence, at his feet, listening to his voice,
receiving his blessing, repeating after him
the words which emancipated them, as they
felt, from sin, sorrow, and temptation.

In a few days, the, I had almost said,
Saint, but as he is not yet canonized by the
Church I may not use the word—in a few
days the Apostle of Temperance had enrolled 150,000 additional members; and here
we may mention that, as few, indeed, of his
clients ever went back, we may make some

faint guess at the amazing amount of good which he effected.

His next visit was to Waterford, where he had been invited by the Right Rev. Dr. Foran, where an immense multitude of people enrolled. Indeed, the success of the Temperance movement now became so great, the members who had joined it so powerful, that it proved injurious to the interest of the distillers, whose breweries were likely to be closed.

It is an eternal credit to Ireland, however, that there were few, indeed, of those men who made a serious opposition to the movement, though in some cases, even an unfair advantage was taken of them. The whiskey-seller wrote to Father Mathew to say that the farmers' sons in his neighborhood, who owed him large sums of money for whiskey, had refused to pay their debts, because they said Father Mathew would not allow them to pay for intoxicating liquors. This was of course a falsehood,

and a very serious one, for the most super-
ficially educated Catholic knows that men
must pay their debts, no matter for what
the debt has been contracted.

It was foolish, also, to argue against the
Temperance movement because a few people suffered from it; as well might it be
argued that men should be allowed to support a druggist's store by buying poisons, as
it would be good for his trade. Besides,
we may never dare to commit sin, and if all
the trade in the world were ruined because
we refrained from one mortal sin ; it would
be better, it would be right, that it should
be ruined.

There was a great deal of idle excuse in
this, too. Selling whiskey, or gin, or cock-
tail, is an easy way, and unhappily a very
sure way of making money. When a man
can make thousands of dollars by an easy
trade, he is not likely to take kindly to one
that will give him a great deal of trouble.
Those spirit-sellers would soon have found

a new occupation which might have brought them in as much money; but it would probably have required more labor to make it pay. Had it been so, they would at least have had their reward in the next world, and that reward would have been permanent, because it will be eternal.

Better to lose a little here, and to gain a great deal hereafter; and better to suffer a good deal here, than to suffer eternal torment; better to suffer the cruelest poverty and the most terrible destitution, than to be the cause or occasion of sin to others.

This was the way in which Father Mathew argued:

What filled our gaols and bridewells? The effects of intoxication. What crowded the very lunatic asylum? Drunkenness and its effects. What fed the very gibbets? Drunkenness. "I never will give up until we are freed, with the blessing and the assistance of God, from all these deplorable evils; and if I encounter, during the prog-

ress of my career, the sneer of some, and
the contumelies of others, I must expect it.
Some there are, and it is strange, look with
an evil eye upon me. But cannot I say in
the words of St. Paul, 'Am I your enemy,
because I tell the truth?' Let them show
me any one brought to gaol or bridewell by
total abstinence? Show me any one sent to
the lunatic asylum from the effects of total
abstinence. Oh, no! not a single one."

In June, 1840, Father Mathew visited
Maynooth, where he enrolled eight professors of the college, 250 students, and 35,000
people. One of the students thus describes
his visit :

"I had the good fortune to be present in
the great hall of the college, when the professors and the students knelt down with
edifying humility under the inspiring eloquence of an humble priest. The scene
was majestically grand; it threw back the
mind upon itself; it drew forth in full light
all that is high, and all that is amiable in

the Irish heart; and to a day-dreamer, like myself, recalled in tender recollection, the memory of other times, and looked for a while like their revival. On an elevated bench, which extended along one side of the quadrangular room, stood the Apostle of Temperance and the judgment to come. The able and amiable Dr. Hughes, Bishop of New York, was present on every occasion, and showed by his feelings, how deeply he loves the land of his birth. Father Mathew was supported on either side by the masters and the professors of the college. The room was piled to the utmost extremity by the students, and several distinguished strangers were occasionally present.

"A small, vacant space, under the bench, was the hallowed spot consecrated to the virtue of temperance. The words of wisdom which he uttered, were followed by deep emotions of joy and astonishment in his audience, and the thunders of involuntary applause that greeted each new acces-

sion of converts, as they moved deliberately
forward in successive files, and with eager
emulation, to the arena of virtue and heroic
self-denial.

" For the more convenient management of
so great an institution, the discipline of the
college wisely separates the senior and
junior parts of the community. The good
man, after his first successful essay in the
senior college, requested to be led to the
junior house. He freely stated the object
of his mission. They listened in silent
wonder; their innocence was startled by
the turpitude of the unfelt gratification, and
their humility was alarmed by the exalted
act of virtue they were invited to imitate.
No postulant appeared, and the holy man
retired with perfect composure, but not
without hope. Their own reflections created
a speedy revolution of sentiment, and they
requested him to return. He hurried with
eager zeal to see them again, and the little
Benjamins, as he endearingly called them,

8

repaid his paternal solicitude by fully emu-
lating, at each successive visit he paid
them, the generous enthusiasm of their se-
niors."

While visiting Maynooth, Father Mathew
was entertained by the Duke of Leinster,
who vied with the professors in doing him
honor. How well the good Father must
have remembered the day when he fled
from that very place in disgrace! How different his return, crowned with honor, the ad-
mired of all, the mighty conqueror! Thus
does humiliation which comes to us from
whatever cause, even if it comes from some
imperfection of our own, become the surest
and the safest way to exaltation, even in
this world; for God gives His grace to
those who humble themselves, and those who
have most of His grace are sure to do most
for Him, and even here they receive from
time to time some little foretaste of their
eternal triumph.

Yet it is but a foretaste, for God loves

His saints too much to allow them uninter
rupted praise, or uninterrupted prosperity.

It was about this time that it became
known that Father Mathew worked miracles. I use the word advisedly, and under
entire submission to the authority of the
Church, which has not yet spoken on the
subject.

All Catholics believe, or ought to believe,
that our Divine Lord left to his disciples, in
such ways, times, and circumstances as He
pleased, the power of working miracles, of
causing certain things to happen which are
directly opposed to what, as far as we know,
are the laws of nature.

This is, for many reasons, an important
subject, and one on which I wish to dwell
a little, and to which I beg your earnest attention. The occurrence from time to time
of miracles is one of the great marks of the
Catholic Church. No one ever heard of a
miracle having happened in a Protestant
sect of any kind. No one ever heard of

any Protestant having performed a miracle.

This is easily explained. No one but God can alter or suspend the laws which God Himself has made, and God does not give the power to work miracles to those who are not Catholics, and no miracles can be worked except by the power of God. Protestants are very fond of talking about what they call the "lying wonders of Popery." They do not believe in miracles. If Christ Himself had performed miracles before their very eyes, they would not have believed Him, and how can they be expected to believe His disciples. But their want of faith does not make these miracles any less true. The sun shines all the same for the blind man, though he sees it not. There are some Protestants invincibly ignorant, so blind that they cannot see. There are some Protestants wilfully ignorant; they will not see.

They are like a man who has good eyesight, and yet shuts his eyes, and says it is all dark, because he does not wish to see. There is no excuse for such persons.

Just as God was pleased to give power to his Apostles to work great miracles, so that, as we read in the Acts of the Holy Apostles, the very *shadow* of St. Peter cured the most terrible diseases, and good Catholics took relics from his very body, handkerchiefs and aprons, and everything they could lay hold of, and then touched the sick with them, so it has ever since been in the Church founded by God on Peter.

From time to time, God has given power to certain holy men and women to work miracles. It is because they love God more, and have been more faithful to Him than others, that He gives them this power. He honors them because they honor Him.

It is as if some great landlord gave power to some faithful steward or servant to do what he liked with his property as a reward for his faithful service.

8*

The steward only works by his master's permission, and all the glory and praise of the good that he does, goes back to his master, so that it is both silly and untrue for Protestants to talk as if it lessened the power or glory of God when the saints work miracles.

The truth is they do not believe God's miracles, and so it is, therefore, no wonder that they do not believe the miracles of God's saints; and as they will not believe, they talk of them as "lying wonders." At the day of judgment they will know where the lie was.

There can be no reasonable doubt that our Father Mathew was one of those holy men to whom God granted the power to heal the sick, and to make the lame walk. I am sorry to say that a Catholic gentleman, who has written his life, has written about all these miracles, as. if they were performed by natural causes; but as these miracles are admitted to be wrought still at

Father Mathew's grave, there can be no doubt that he had obtained the power or gift from God.

A Protestant doctor with whom Father Mathew was very intimate, has fully admitted, that Father Mathew *did* effect cures by his prayers, which were above the power of living men, which could not be effected by mortal means; but he tries to persuade his friends, as he tried to persuade himself, that they were caused by mesmerism or animal magnetism, and further gravely adds that they were the cause of Father Mathew's death.

If Father Mathew had died young, there might have been some excuse for this assertion; but he lived to a good old age, and the wonder is, not that he died when he did, but that he lived so long, when we consider what a life he led of incessant toil and labor. But the Protestant doctor did not attempt to account for the serious fact that many of the most remarkable of Father

Mathew's miracles were performed at his grave, where he certainly could not mesmerize any one.

Such unbelief is excusable in a Protestant, but it is very pitiable in a Catholic. It is true, indeed, that the devil has great power, that he has all the power and craft of a fallen angel, and that God permits him occasionally to deceive people by false miracles, by making his followers do some things, which, to a certain extent are wonderful, because they are above our mortal powers. But he can only go so far as God lets him; and it is certain the one-half of the wonderful things that are told of spirit-rappers and mediums turns out lies; while the more you ‾investigate the miracles performed by God's saints, the more their truth is manifested.

And here I may observe, in passing, that the reason why the Church takes such care to examine all the miracles said to have been performed by a person, before he is canonized, shows how careful the Church is to discern the true from the false, and, further, that the Church is the only guide, in such matters, of what is true and what is false, because the saints work the miracles by the power of God, and the Church decides by the authority of God.

Therefore, until any person is canonized or determined by the Church to have been a saint, we can only take his or her miracles on credit. But there is this difference between a Protestant and a Catholic in such matters; a Catholic, when he hears that any priest or holy person has performed miracles, is inclined to believe them, does not doubt that they may be true, and, if he finds, on inquiring, that they are true, he gives God glory; and this we ought to do with regard to the miracles worked by Father Mathew; while a Protestant at once denies and disputes without a single inquiry.

CHAPTER VII.

Father Mathew and the reporters — A "model" young man —
Confusion of reporter who had broken the pledge — Father
Mathew hears a conversation not complimentary to himself — He visits the North of Ireland — He is well received
by the Orangemen — His wonderful spirit of charity.

ATHER MATHEW'S speeches,
and accounts of his meetings, were
now regularly reported in the papers
and, of course, above all, in the Cork papers.
The reporters were all well-known to him;
indeed he was especially active in canvassing
among them for postulants, for the young
men, as he well knew, would be the future
and the most efficient supporters of his great
work.

The good friar was especially attached to
one of the reporters, named L——, who
reciprocated his affection. On one occasion,
L—— went down to Fermoy, to report

(94)

a great demonstration; and he put up at
the same hotel with Father Mathew. Poor
L—— was not remarkable for his strength
of mind or tenacity of purpose, and yield-
ing either to the weakness of his nature, or
the solicitations of his more sceptical friends,
to use the popular phrase of the day, he
"broke the pledge;" he, however, insisted
he had only surrendered it. At any rate,
he was not then a "teetotaller," though he
did not think it necessary to apprise his
friend Father Mathew of that fact. L——
was at his little table on the platform, working diligently with the pencil some times,
and taking his leisure at others as some well
remembered passage was repeated by the
speaker. Father Mathew was urging on
his hearers the fact that no one had suffered
in health or pocket from having taken his
advice; and, happening to glance at L——'s
handsome face, he found, as he believed, a
happy illustration of the health which the
"steadfast teetotaller" was sure to obtain

and retain; and placing his hand fondly on the head of the horrified L——, he thus continued, to his victim's ineffable confusion: "Look, my dear friends! here is a fine specimen of a faithful teetotaller (L—— blushing deeply); he never tastes anything stronger than water or tea (L——'s confusion increasing). There is the hue of health on his countenance—not the flush of strong drink (L—— red as a peony, and his pencil paralyzed). He, my dear friends, will never, please God, barter his moral independence for a fleeting gratification. He will not be like Esau, who sold his birthright for a mess of pottage (L—— wishing devoutly that the ground might open and swallow him, or that, at the very least, some accident might happen to the platform). No, my dear people, my young friend here, is a faithful follower of the cause, and will never turn his back on the pure and spotless banner." Fortunately, here the personal allusion ceased, and the fondling hand was taken from the head of the victim; for, had the torture continued longer, as L—— afterwards assured his friends, something dreadful would have happened him. It was, however, not all over with him yet. Father Mathew and L—— breakfasted the next morning at the same table. During breakfast, L—— desired the waiter to bring his bill. "Oh, no, my dear," said Father Mathew, "you are my guest here; you must not pay anything." "Thank you, sir, not at all—I assure you I must pay my own bill. Waiter, bring it to me at once." "Waiter, do no such thing; everything must be included in mine. I could not think of allowing it." L—— made a last desperate effort—"I assure you, Father Mathew, Mr. —— (the proprietor of the journal he represented) would be very indignant with me, if I allowed you to pay my bill. Waiter, bring it to me." "Do what I desire, waiter," said Father Mathew, with a manner that was not to be disputed.

Ω

L—— looked at the waiter, and the waiter looked at L——, and L——'s glance of despair was only matched by the waiter's look of comical perplexity.   Before the document, respecting which this struggle took place, was produced, L—— was seated on Bian ;* his back turned to the hotel. During the previous evening and night, poor L—— had sought consolation in rather deep potations; and, in the bill which was thrust into the pocket of the Apostle of Temperance, there was a fearful list of "materials" for whiskey-punch and " goes " of brandy and water!   For a month after, L—— fled from the face of Father Mathew; but, when they afterwards met, the latter did not, by the slightest sign, exhibit his knowledge of the fact that poor weak L—— had sold his birthright for a mess of pottage.

It was somewhat about the same time that two members of the Cork press were sent to an important meeting of the same

---

* A popular abbreviation for Bianconi's car.

character. Having performed their duty, they immediately drove to a distant village at which the night mail was to stop, and in which they had taken their seats; here they dined, and then wrote out their report. At the appointed time the mail arrived, and they occupied their places. There was but one other inside passenger, and he was muffled up in a corner, and was quite silent, and was supposed by the friends to be indulging in a comfortable nap. The friends, as soon as they were well settled, commenced a lively chat. At length one asked the other this question: "Jack, what do you think Father Mathew is doing now?" "What is he doing? Why, taking a good stiff tumbler of punch, such as you and I, Dick, will take, please the Fates, at the next stage." "Punch! Nonsense, man; surely you are jesting. You don't think Father Mathew is such a hypocrite?" "Faith, I don't care what he is, my boy; but I am sure the jolly old buffer is taking a stiff tumbler at this

moment—and I wish I had the same."
When the coach arrived at the next stage,
the gentlemen of the press got out, and,
entering the inn, called for the promised
beverage.   They had got through about
half of their smoking tumblers, when the
guard entered, saying, " Come gentlemen,
time is up; please make haste."   " Halloo,
guard!" said Jack, the more convivial of
the two, " take something."   " I thank you
kindly, sir, no—I am temperate."   " You,
coachman — won't you have a drop this
cold night?"   " No, sir; thank you all the
same.   I hav'n't tasted anything for years,
and, please God, I never will.   But I am as
much obliged to you, sir, as if I took what's
in the house."   " Tell me, guard, who is
that you have in the coach with us?"
" Don't you know him, sir?   He's one the
country ought to be proud of.   It's Father
Mathew!"   It is not necessary to represent,
with accuracy, the exclamations uttered by
the doubter of the consistency of the temper-

ance leader; it is enough to say, that he precipitately abandoned the remainder of his punch, and, scrambling up to a seat behind the coachman, thus accomplished the rest of his journey. The other, on entering the coach, received a warm shake of the hand; but, not a word was said by Father Mathew of the conversation, which he no doubt fully heard, for he asked where was Mr. ——; to which the reply was made, that the inside of the coach did not agree with him, and that he preferred the fresh air. The sceptic must certainly have been peculiar in taste, for the night was frightfully cold.

Father Mathew was invited to the North of Ireland by the Right Rev. Dr. Blake, the late Catholic Bishop of Dromore, whom the good friar used to describe as "that Bishop after St. Paul's own heart." The writer of this work had also the honor of knowing this excellent prelate; and, as long as life shall last, the memory of his winning smile,

9*

nis bright keen eye, and the warm affection he showed to her, must remain as one of her dearest memories.   .

Father Mathew himself gave an account, at the meeting in Newry, of how he was received in the Protestant North. He had been warned, before setting out, that he would be assassinated if he went there, for party feud ran high, and a leading Catholic would of course be an object of dislike to many. But, for the credit of Ireland, no such crime seemed ever likely to happen, and Father Mathew himself said afterwards, in the words of the poet, slightly altered:

> "Blessed be forever the day I relied
> On Ulster's honor, and Ulster's pride."

The good priest was, indeed, gifted with a very great degree of what, for want of a better or more expressive word, we must call "tact;" and yet what looked like tact, what would have been merely tact or worldly policy in a less religious person, was probably in him but an overflowing of Christian charity.

This charity not only bears all things, and hopes all things, but it also suffers all things; and the happy possessor of this gift will even persuade himself that, what others might think an insult, has been intended for a kindness. It was in this spirit, certainly, that Father Mathew accepted a display of orange flags as a personal compliment.

"At Clones," he said, in one of his speeches, "there were two orange flags raised when I visited it, and instead of an insult, I thought them a very great compliment, never having seen one, or been honored with one before; and the Catholics and Protestants became the greatest friends, from that day forward; and during three days, while I remained there, the parties were the best friends imaginable." This is, indeed, a proof, if proof were needed, that it only requires a little exercise of prudence and Christian charity on both sides, to make Irishmen unite in one common bond, however much they may have differed on religion or politics. Theirs will surely be a bright reward, who prevent or decrease these bitter feuds, which ought, for every reason, to be buried in oblivion.

CHAPTER VIII.

ATHER MATHEW had now reached the very zenith of his fame; not, indeed, that fame was what he desired, or was even in itself desirable to his noble heart; still his personal reputation had helped his work, and he might rejoice in that, since his work was all for God. But he was not without his trials, as we have said before. What true servant of God has ever been free from the Cross? His personal expenses were necessarily very great, or, perhaps, we should have said,

(105)

more correctly, his relative expenses. His own private expenses were few as ever; no one could have lived or clothed himself more poorly, with the common respect due to his position as a priest; but his public expenses were now increasing daily.

Mr. Purcell and Mr. Bianconi had given him a free pass for all their public cars, and these were then the principal modes of conveyance in Ireland; but this did not serve him much. He could not bear to see poverty without relieving it, and he could not travel far in poor Ireland without encountering the greatest want in every village and at every town.

Again, he was constantly asked to preach for some charity. It is true that he was not what would be called a fine preacher according to modern ideas, but he was none the less—perhaps it would be more correct to say he was all the more, attractive, all the more successful. He was full of his subject, he thought nothing of himself, he did not seek to make an impression; and if he did not fail to make one, it was because he made it unconsciously from his very earnestness.

He could not preach for a charity without helping it, and as it was known that he had received one or two considerable donations for the Temperance cause from wealthy English gentlemen, it was concluded that he was the possessor of, or at least had the key to untold coffers of gold.

' In truth, these noblemen, with all their apparent liberality, did but give, for them, a mere trifle, a trifle which they had, perhaps, expended hundreds of times on some sinful or selfish gratification.

Then; again, his very liberality led to false impressions; for few could understand how any man would give away his last shilling, not once or twice, but fifty or a hundred times over. He was, indeed, a living example of the holy poverty which he had vowed on entering the Franciscan Or-

der; and though he was at times greatly
tried, as the poor must be, for their greater
merit, and the enhancement of their crown,
he was also greatly blessed; and it seemed
that the more he gave away the more he
had to give.   '

The Temperance bands were also a
source of great expense to him.   Each town
and society had its own band; this was but
right, and was a valuable assistance to the
cause.   Some one has said that we ought
not to let the devil have all the good things
for himself, and I am sure that if more
pains were taken by good people to make
religion pleasant, that there would be less
temptations to sin for the weak and weary,
and perhaps a better chance of perseverance
even for the strong.

One thing at least is certain, that there
were new bands formed for each society,
that bands cost money, and that Father
Mathew was generally, and not unsuccess-
fully, applied to for help.   Each society, of

course, only thought of its own necessities, which seemed to it the most pressing ; each constantly expected help ; and good Father Mathew was only too willing to give the help to each and all, as far as he could, and even more than he could.

The drum was always the great feature in these bands, and the drummer, of course, the principal person. Many rare anecdotes were told of Father Mathew's drummers, and the powers they exhibited on important occasions. The strongest men were supposed to be the best drummers, since force was considered the best qualification for producing sound, and sound was the one thing to be desired.

Happily for himself, Father Mathew did not know one note of music ; but what he could understand was sound ; so he and the drummers were excellent friends, and they received all the praise they deserved and merited. But they obtained something more. At the conclusion of the Temper-

10

ance tea-party, or picnic, 'or meeting, as
the case might be, the great leader generally sent "something" to the band, as a
compliment for their performance and an
encouragement to perseverance.   There
were necessarily many calls of this kind on
his purse ; what wonder, then, if it was
generally empty, however often any friendly
hand might replenish it?

Of course, Father Mathew was accused
of having ulterior political designs in his
Temperance movement.   There are some
ignorant and hopelessly prejudiced individuals in what are called the highest ranks of
life, as well as in the lowest; and where any
Irish or Catholic movement is concerned,
they seem to lose even any little sense that
nature has kindly bestowed on them.

But this was not all; persons, who
probably were seldom seen in any place of
worship, and who certainly never tried to
avert the thousand evils of sinful Sabbath-
breaking, by which many English towns

are made hideous, cried out, long and loud, and with much elevating of eyebrows and frequent sighs of pious horror, concerning the innocent amusements in which he encouraged the people, after their religious duties were fulfilled, on Sundays.

He replied thus to those bigoted calumniators: "There are difficulties which cause me more pain than the assertion of Sir Robert Peel—the insidious efforts to give to our society a political coloring, and to invoke a gloomy fanatical cry against us. The great body of teetotallers, it is true, is composed of Roman Catholics; but that is from the great bulk of the people being Roman Catholics, and not from anything exclusive in our society. A hostile disposition has been excited on this account in certain localities; and I must, also, complain, with the deepest sorrow, that many who, from rank and station, possess great influence, have not, to use the mildest terms, exercised it in favor of our society.

"I utterly disclaim any political object; my ardent desire is to promote the glory of God by drying up the fruitful source of crime, and the happiness of His creatures by persuading them to the observance of temperance.

"Our musical bands, too, and our processions, are rocks of offence to many. If it was allowed to any to object to them, surely it should be to the members of your society [The Friends], who reject music and parade, in every case; yet, you have all magnanimously coöperated with me, despising the paltry pretext. I respect the religious feelings which disapprove of music and processions on the Lord's Day; I would not, on any account, offer violence to tender consciences; but we, Roman Catholics, after in general devoting the afternoon of Saturday, and the forenoon of Sunday, to religious observances, do not deem it a desecration of the Sabbath, for such as have been earning their bread by the sweat of their brows during the week, to recreate themselves innocently during the remainder of the day."

Father Mathew's naturally strong constitution enabled him to get through an amount of work which few other men could have attempted. Indeed, we cannot doubt that God, who orders all things for His people, had given him this almost exceptional strength, as it was certainly necessary for the great work to which he was called. The following record, taken from a Cork paper, will give some idea of the extent and energy of his labors :

" Father Mathew left Cork on Saturday, August the 10th, for Newmarket, where he was to preach yesterday the 11th, and afterwards to administer the pledge. Of course, every one was desirous of seeing him, and, of course, all means were considered justifiable that tended to so very desirable an end. On one occasion, he had arrived in the dusk of the evening at the house of a parish priest in the remotest part

10*

of Galway, where he was to preach in aid
of the funds of a school, convent or chapel,
and afterwards administer the pledge.   The
best room in the house was prepared for
the honored guest, who was conducted
to it by his host.   The room was on the
ground floor, and was lighted by a large
bay window, which was without blind or
curtain of any kind.   Father Mathew, whose
bedroom in Cove street, was as plain and
simple as this apartment, only thought of
preparing himself, by a good night's rest,
for the labors of the following day; and,
turning his face to the wall, and his back to
the window, he soon fell into a deep slumber.
Awaking, as was usual with him, at an early
hour in the morning, he opened his eyes,
blessed himself, repeated a prayer, and
turned towards the window.   But, imagine
his dismay, when he beheld a crowd of
people—men, women and children, in front
of the blindless and curtainless bay-window,
and at least a score of noses flattened against

the glass, the better to enable their respective proprietors to obtain a peep at his reverence. A more modest man did not exist than Father Mathew; and great was his embarrassment at this indication of his popularity.' He glanced at the head of the bed, and at the table near him, to see if a bell were in reach; but such a luxury in the house of a priest, in a mountain parish of Galway, was not to be thought of. No help, therefore, from that quarter. There was something resembling a bell-pull near the fire-place, but if not a mockery and a delusion, it might as well have been twenty miles away, for any practical advantage at that moment; for it would be difficult to say what would induce Father Mathew to quit the shelter of the bed-clothes, and walk across the room to grasp that tantalizing cord.

" The crowd outside was momentarily on the increase, and the deepening murmur of their voices testified to the animation of

the conversation carried on. Occasionally
might be heard such as the following : 'Do
ye see him, Mary, astore?' 'Danny, agra,
lave me take a look, an' God bless you,
child!' 'Where are you pushing with yer-
self? Hould off ov my foot, will ye?' 'Oh,
wisha! There is the blessed priest?' 'Honest
man, would ye be plazed to lift off ov our
back—one 'ud think 'tis a horse I was.' 'Tis
a shame for ye to be there—what curosity
is in yes all!' 'Mammy, mammy! there he
is!—I sees his poll!' 'Whisht, an' don't be
after wakin' him.' Father Mathew ventured
another peep; but the slightest movement
on his part only evoked increased anxiety
outside; and it seemed to him as if the win-
dow-pains were every moment accommo-
dating a larger number of flattened noses.
The poor man felt himself a prisoner, and
listened with eagerness for any sound which
gave hope or promise of deliverance; but
it was not till after three mortal hours of
his guest's comical captivity that the con-

siderate host, who would not disturb his guest too early, entered the apartment, and thus became aware of the presence of the admiring crowd, who, it need scarcely be said, were quickly dispersed, to Father Mathew's ineffable relief."

Father Mathew saw many and many a pitiable exhibition of the fearful effects of intemperance, and he knew that to save young souls from the ruin which it involves, was to them the greatest favor, to God the greatest glory. He left no effort unused to win the young, to encourage them to join his societies, to assist them to persevere when the first step had been taken.

He loved his native land, and he loved his people, and he knew well that that land would be a by-word and a reproach while it lay enslaved in the chains of a degrading vice; that its people never could be free until they had learned to respect themselves, and to make others respect them.

Crime had already decreased; for the

Irishman rarely commits a crime, except under the influence of the demon Drink. Even the judges, as they went circuit, proclaimed the great effects of this man's work, as represented in the decrease of criminal cases; while those witnesses who came into court with a Temperance medal were seen to be heard with special attention.

In the year 1839, no less than 12,049 persons had been committed for various offences. In 1845, there were only 7,101 criminals. In 1839, sixty-six persons were sentenced to death ; while in 1845 there were only thirteen. And this decrease was steady, year by year showing the number happily less, as, year by year, the people of Ireland learned that the demon Drink was their cruelest enemy, and obtained, by Divine grace, strength to resist it effectually.

The returns of the number of gallons of whisky on which duty was paid are also another item in the calculation of the good effected. In 1839 there was duty paid to

the amount of £1,434,573 ; in 1844 the duty
paid was reduced to £852,418; at the same
time, and as a happy consequence, the con-
sumption of tea and sugar greatly increased.

It is, certainly, amazing, when we consider
the amount of money expended on what
was not even a luxury or a necessity, but a
vile poison ; for, while persons belonging to
the upper classes, may obtain unadulterated
wines or spirits, it has been proved over
and over again that the most poisonous and
deleterious compounds are sold to the poor,
and are taken by them, and are paid for by
them. If one-half this amount were spent
on good food and good clothes, there would
be less necessity for emigration, and more
encouragement for the best kind of industry
in Ireland.

A man who spends all his earnings, or
even any considerable part of them, in the
public-house, is an enemy to his country, as
well as to himself. He is also an enemy to

the publican, for he is encouraging him to invest money in a trade—rather, I should say, in an occupation, that generally leads to ruin; and even if, for a time, he seems to prosper, it will be only for a time, for no real or perfect prosperity ever comes, even in this world, to those who live on the sin of others; and what should we say of the future—what shall we say of the judgment which God shall pass on them?

My friends, let no boy of yours either patronize or keep a liquor store. If you are so unhappy as to be in the position of keeping a liquor store, get rid of it as soon as you can, and get into some business where you can make honest money without being either directly or indirectly the occasion of sin to your fellow-creatures.

Be assured that God will reward you, even in this world, for any sacrifice you have made for his love. And even should you suffer some temporal loss, it will be more than compensated to you when you are in eternity.

Father Mathew had to contend with the complaints of those who declared that he had ruined their trade, as we have seen ; and even some members of his own family suffered; still he did not hesitate in his course for a moment. Why should he? What profit would it be to his family if they gained thousands by the sins of others, and then lost their own souls, or had the heavy guilt of being accessory to the sin of others.

He spoke thus on this important subject in December, 1842 :

" I do not know but that there are distillers or brewers listening to me. One member of my family in Cashel, a distiller. now manufactures, I am glad to say, as much in a week as would supply his customers for a year. This is a great falling off from other days. I am rejoiced at this, for when the glory of God is in question, we should not mind the ties of flesh and blood."

Miss Edgeworth, the well-known novelist, bears ardent testimony to the necessity

11

of Father Mathew's mission. She lived at the village of Edgeworthstown, in the County Longford, and well describes the difference between the state of that place when nearly every man was a drunkard, and its state when nearly every man was sober. She describes the joy and peace of the wife who found once more her husband's love and support, the children well clothed and happy, and the father himself, rejoicing in the mighty change, and wondering how he had ever been such a fool as to have lived as he once did, more like a brute than a Christian.

Cardinal Wiseman, also, that great and good man, from whom we ourselves, at his own desire, received the holy sacrament of Confirmation, preached a panegyric on the "holy son of St. Francis," as he fittingly described Father Mathew.

CHAPTER IX.

Father Mathew a true hero — His fame will be eternal — His trials with those who broke the pledge — Thackeray's opinion of him — Father Mathew avoids politics — The reason of this — He assists the Repeal movement unconsiously by making the people sober — O'Connell announces his intention to walk in the Cork procession — Magnificent demonstration at which O'Connell assists — The Mayor kneels at the end in the public street to receive Father Mathew's blessing.

HE great movement began now to attract attention in America. Dr. Channing, of that country, said: "History records no revolution like this; it is the great work of the present day. Father Mathew, the leader of this moral revolution, ranks far above heroes and statesmen of the times. This was, indeed, true, and a remarkable admission from a Protestant minister; for truly the fame of the world's great men is but for the present, save in these few instances, when

the first object of the hero is the glory of God, and when he works for the glory of God as well as for earthly honor or earthly renown.

Father Mathew rarely or never lost his temper; and that is saying a good deal for him when we consider the life he led. Only those who are obliged to live active lives of incessant occupation, of ceaseless care, of continual labor; lives which allow nothing to nature beyond what is absolutely necessary, which give but rare moments for rest and none for actual pleasures ;• only such persons can understand the difficulty of possessing a perfect equanimity of temper.

Father Mathew's heart was in his cause, and we may be assured that, if it had not been, his cause would never have prospered as it did. It may be very amusing for those who are in earnest in nothing but in sin, to sneer at those who are in earnest for God : but their mirth will not profit them much. When the devil can do nothing else, when he has in

vain fought with an earnest and holy soul,
when he has in vain tried to hinder a holy
work by other means, he tries the weapons
of ridicule or contempt, to disgust the object
of that contempt by the very device which
he has himself suggested.

If nothing else will do, he will attack the
poor soul when weary—body and mind, and
will try to destroy the holiest effects by some
act of impatience or disgust.

Father Mathew's one great trial was when
any of his disciples broke the pledge. There
were few, indeed, who proved unfaithful ; so
very few, indeed, that it seems almost miraculous, almost supernatural ; for in truth it
was above and beyond the power of nature,
that so many should have been faithful, and
so very, very few should have yielded to the
strong temptation.

But what tried him most of all was a deliberate renunciation of the pledge. There
might be some failures through the country,
of which, of course, he would never hear ;

11*

but there is ample public testimony to show how few these failures were. Now and then, however, some disciple would come to him with deliberate purpose, and declare his inability to refrain from the temptation any longer.

One individual unfortunately tried his temper. He came to Father Mathew, and assured him that he could no longer take the lemonade, which he had substituted for punch, after dinner. Father Mathew advised water, but that was not to be thought of. He advised tea or coffee, the latter being, indeed, a most pleasant and palatable after-dinner beverage; but no, the gentleman had come to resign the pledge, and he was not to be coaxed or caressed into keeping it.

He declared that he only took one tumbler of punch after dinner, but one he must have.

Father Mathew, who knew very well the danger of "only one glass," turned to him with a holy indignation and exclaimed, " Then, sir, you may go and drink a bucket-full of it every day of your life."

Some amusing scenes are said to have occurred when countrymen came, now and then, to return the pledge. Poor fellows! they had not conscience enough, or strength of mind enough, to keep themselves from temptation ; and they had just faith enough not to like to break their vow. They fancied they could free themselves by giving back the medal, but this was easier said than done. Father Mathew began to understand the state of the case, after one or two attempts, and quietly treated the vacillating individual as if he had come for no other purpose than to take the vow he really intended to break.

The poor countryman would be " taken a-back," and would begin to explain " that it was all for the good of his health " that he wanted to be freed from his vow. But Father Mathew had a stock of arguments ready, and when they failed he would have recourse to something very like physical force; a hearty shake, a good scolding, positive refusal to take back the medal, was generally found effectual. Now and then, however, some individual, who was determined to go to the devil without let or hinderance, would fling in his medal and slam to the door, and then take to his heels down the street.

Poor fellow! How the demon must have laughed and shouted to see him run! It was as if he held the key of Paradise in his hand, and flung it away lest he should succeed in entering therein. Only God and the holy angels could know the danger of that man. The barriers once broken down, the great safeguard once removed, his ruin was sure; for rarely indeed would he again reform.

Once the summary method of getting rid of the pledge was discovered, a perfect remedy was applied, as far as Cork was concerned; for Father Mathew was rarely without two or three faithful disciples, and they were ready and willing to pounce forth on the flying individual, who hoped to escape by his fleetness of foot. An exciting chase was the usual result of every surreptitious attempt to return the medal, and the depositor was generally captured, and, after a suitable lecture and effectual persuasion, was induced to take up his medal once more.

In the year 1842, the good Father received a very gratifying letter from the Catholic Bishop of Madras, who told him that a whole company of soldiers had come to him "to be enrolled in Father Mathew's society." Letters such as this, and the holy friar received many such, were no little consolation to him in his life of weary labor. As his biographer truly says, it was not because they gratified his vanity, for that he had long since tried to subdue and mortify; had he not done so, he could scarcely have prospered as he did in his work; but it was because they consoled his heart.

The very affectionateness of his disposition
led him to desire sympathy ardently, and to
shrink painfully from the least unkindness.
But his goodness of heart shielded him
from all but the malicious few, who find, in
the prosperity of any individual, a sufficient
reason for despising his work or himself.
Even the cynical Thackeray had a good
word for the Irish *soggarth*, and writes of
him in terms of warm commendation.

" There is nothing remarkable," he says,
" in Mr. Mathew's manner, except that it
is exceedingly simple, hearty and manly.
With the state of the country, of landlord,
tenant and peasantry, he seems to be most
curiously and entirely acquainted; his
knowledge of the people is prodigious, and
their confidence in him is great; and what
a touching attachment that is, which these
poor fellows show to any one who has their
cause at heart, even to any one who says he
has ! One of his disciples, in a livery coat,
came into the room with a tray; Mr.

Mathew recognized him and shook him by the hand directly; so he did with the strangers that were presented to him, and not with a courtly, popularity-hunting air, but, as it seemed, from sheer hearty kindness and a desire to do every one good."

His " desire to do every one good," which struck the Englishman so much, was just the very key-note of the harmony of Father Mathew's life, and the source of his success. Still, while the half-heathen Thackeray very naturally took the lowest view of his motives, and attributed all to mere benevolence, we know that his " desire to do every one good " had a far higher motive.

Mere human benevolence may lead a man to do much for his fellow-creatures, if he can do it without any serious personal inconvenience; it needs the constraining power of the love of God to induce and to enable a man to sacrifice his time, his comfort in life, his whole being, as Father Mathew sacrificed his, for the sake of his fellow men.

Mr. Thackeray also explained that " Mr."
Mathew, as he was pleased to call him,
seemed to have no political opinions. O'Connell's agitation was in full action, and its success was admittedly and undoubtedly mainly
attributable to the Temperance movement.
But Father Mathew, with the most consummate prudence, kept himself even from any
appearance of joining in the proceedings. He
knew well that his agitation must be purely
spiritual, if it was to succeed ; and he wished
to unite all classes and all creeds, as well as
all shades of political opinion, in the one
great effort to regenerate the country.

But O'Connell well knew the value of
Father Mathew's passive coöperation, and
did all that he possibly could to encourage
his followers to join the Temperance movement. If a proof were needed that Irishmen
only require to be sober, to gain all that
they desire, that proof was given.

On Easter morning, March 28th, 1842,
O'Connell joined the Temperance procession

himself in Cork, no doubt with the view of impressing the value of the society more strongly on his followers. He announced his intention on the previous Monday, at the weekly meeting in Conciliation Hall. This arrangement was not altogether satisfactory to Father Mathew, as it looked too much like a personal sanction of a certain line of political action. But he had no choice, and the event proved that there need have been no apprehension.

A procession of some ten thousand people marched that day in Cork, and it was one of the most impressing Temperance demonstrations ever witnessed. The following account is from the Cork " Examiner " of that day :

" From an early hour in the morning, which was rather threatening, and inclined to rain, the city was thronged with numberless crowds of people, either anxious to behold the anticipated spectacle, or about to fall in with the several societies that were

12

to walk on the occasion. Every road, street, lane and avenue, leading into Cork, echoed to the sound of music, as hundreds and thousands poured in from neighboring towns and districts of the country, or even from places so far distant as thirty or forty miles. Long before the time appointed for starting, the vast area of the Corn-market was densely crowded with various societies, each headed by its band of twenty or thirty musicians, the members dressed with scarfs, blue, pink or green, of Irish manufacture, and holding a long white wand decorated with colored ribbon or laurel. Before the several societies was borne a flag or banner, generally with the name of the particular town to which they belonged ; some having painted on them an appropriate device, or allegorical representation, and in many cases a full length figure of the Apostle himself.

" At the hour of eleven, the procession began to move slowly from the Corn-market, over Anglesea Bridge, along the Parade, and

up Great George street, the Western road,
and so through the entire route settled on
some weeks previously. When they had
proceeded as far as the County Club-House,
they were met by the Lord Mayor of Dublin, who came to join Father Mathew; their
greeting was warm and affectionate.

" The scene which followed, it might be
possible to imagine, but is certainly impossible to describe. Who could tell of the wild
joyous shout that rent the very air, as the
two great men of Ireland, the political and
the moral emancipators of her people, met
together ; the eagerness ; the exclamations
of delight; the rushing forward to snatch a
look at both? The rapture and enthusiasm
of that moment, are beyond our poor powers of description. In a short time after,
Thomas Lyons, our own mayor, accompan-
ied by several respectable gentlemen and
merchants, joined the procession. Another
shout welcomed his arrival. Father Mathew
then walked, with the Lord Mayor on one

side, and the Mayor of Cork on the other. Every window was crowded with brilliant groups of fashionably dressed ladies, who waved their handkerchiefs as the splendid array filed before them. Every roof, hall-door, balcony, balustrade, wall, and projection, was literally covered with a mass of eager and delighted beings. who cheered with all their might as the Liberator or Apostle came in view. As the procession was passing the house of Dr. Bullen, on the South Mall, in a window of which sat the Right Reverend Dr. Murphy, the leaders halted, whereupon every man raised his hat, in respect for our venerable and beloved bishop, while loud and continued cheers echoed from ten thousand voices. His lordship, who seemed visibly affected at this testimony of affectionate respect, blessed the thousands before him, and bowed with an appearance of great feeling. No language can at all do justice to the tremendous crowd of people who did not form part of the regular array, but who lined the streets on both sides, and who required all the exertions of the vigorous stewards to keep them from breaking the line of march. In whatever street there was a Temperance reading-room, there was an arch of green boughs, spanning its breadth from house to house. Banners, emblems, garlands of flowers, paintings of various kinds, busts of Father Mathew, and allegorical devices decorated the walls and windows of the several rooms before which the procession passed.

" The Lord Mayor separated from the procession at the end of Lancaster Quay, when he knelt down and received the blessing of Father Mathew, amidst the rapturous cheerings of the countless spectators. His lordship then departed, in company with the Mayor of Cork.

" After marching through the various streets marked out by the managing committee, the vast body of the people arrived at

12*

the terminus, the Corn market, about three
o'clock, when, after having cheered several
times, they quietly separated with the most
admirable order."

CHAPTER X.

Father Mathew visits Glasgow — He receives an address there from Protestants — His miraculous powers — Wonderful effect on Mr. O'C—— — How he made him actually dislike spirits — His reception on his return to Ireland — Amusing story about his brother John.

ATHER MATHEW had often been asked to extend the sphere of his labors, and especially to visit Scotland, where so many of his countrymen were located; but he loved Ireland too much to labor elsewhere, at least until the Temperance movement had been firmly established in that country. At last he complied with one of the many invitations; and in August, 1842, he landed in Greenock, and the same evening arrived in Glasgow.

On the following day, August 14th, and

the eve of the Assumption of our Blessed
Lady, he preached to an immense congre-
gation, and, shortly after, he begun to administer the pledge.

On the 16th of August his arrival was
celebrated by a monster procession, in which
he rejoiced, not because of any honor done to ·
himself personally, but because it was a means,
and a most effectual one, of making his work
more widely known, and of extending that
enthusiasm which is so necessary, or rather
so useful, for the success of any great undertaking.

Even at the very moment when it might
have been supposed that he would enjoy
such rest as could be had in a procession,
and all the honor which thousands were
vieing with each other in rendering to him,
his Master's work was his one great object.
It was found that he had slipped quietly
away from the carriage and the procession, from the rest, and from the honors,
and had retired to the Cattle-market, where

were assembled some poor fellows who were anxious to take the pledge, and could not wait until the conclusion of the procession.

Truly, on all occasions, it was God and souls first, and Father Mathew's rest last. And he has his reward now. He is honored for-ever and forever, where no trail of envy can dare to throw a shade upon his fame, where no unkindness can grieve his gentle heart, where he rests forever and forever, where he shall rest for countless ages in the eternal peace of God.

There was a Temperance banquet at the close of the day, where Father Mathew came to do more work for God. An ad-dress was read to him, amid the acclama-tions of hundreds of Protestants, and the address was presented by a Protestant. His reply, like himself, was full of Divine chari-ty. He spoke still of love—for his heart was full of it, of charity to God, and of charity to the neighbor; and, in truth, his life was an exemplification of his holy words.

A Protestant paper thus describes his work :

" On Monday, Father Mathew administered the pledge to from 1,000 to 1,500; and on Tuesday, after the great procession was over, not fewer than 10,000 to 12,000 people were enlisted in the teetotal cause. Wednesday, however, the number of applicants was so immense, that all attempts at calculation must be set aside. In the morning Father Mathew celebrated mass in the Catholic Chapel, Clyde Street, and afterwards proceeded to the Cattle-market, where a vast concourse of people was assembled. Indeed, the great square of the market was, at one period of the day, so crowded, that it was scarcely possible for the most vigorous to push their way through, and many who ardently longed for an opportunity of kneeling before the great Apostle of Temperance, and taking the pledge from his lips, could not get even a sight of his face. Late in the afternoon, he saw females who had anxiously waited the whole day, in the hope of being able to get near his person, but were disappointed, and we understand that great numbers were similarly circumstanced at the close of the proceedings. From ten o'clock, A.M., till six o'clock, Father Mathew was laboriously employed in administering the pledge, and as the day was excessively hot, his exertions must have been attended with great fatigue. Group after group was pledged during the whole of the day, to the number of many thousands; but from the pressure it was impossible to keep any account—it is impossible, as we have already remarked, even to guess at the gross number. Such of the people as were previously in the possession of tickets or medals, put them into his hands, and he returned them, throwing the ribbons by which they were suspended over the necks of the owners. In the Catholic Chapel, yesterday morning, he distinctly informed the audience, that he arrogated to himself no

power of performing miracles or cur-
ing diseases, and that any one who ap-
proached him under such a delusion must
be signally disappointed, the power of
performing miracles belonging alone to the
Supreme Being. He, however, stated that
he was willing and ready to bestow his
blessing on all who chose to seek it. Notwithstanding these disclaimers, however,
crowds of diseased persons were taken to the
Cattle-market. At the close of the proceedings, yesterday, Father Mathew appeared
to be quite exhausted by his labors."

In this age of scepticism, we must say a
word of Father Mathew's reiterated dis-
claimer of the power of working miracles.
As we have already said, the Church has
not yet spoken on the subject, therefore we
may not speak of the miracles wrought by
him, as we would do of the miracles wrought
by a canonized Saint. But this does not
make his miracles any the less true. There
is ample reason to believe that he did

work cures beyond the power of medical skill.

I myself know the gentleman to whom the circumstances happened which I shall now record; he is still living, though at a very advanced age.

My friend, who then lived in Killarney, had a very large business as a timber merchant. He was a young man of promise, and of great and earnest nationality; he had married very young, and was still young, though he was the father of twelve children, the eldest of whom was only fourteen years of age. Mr. O'C——'s wife had just died, and his warm, affectionate heart was deeply tried.

Business, however, should go on, and he had arranged with some friends to go to Cork. It was a long journey from Killarney in those days, but it was safely made. The gentlemen went about their different occupations the next day after their arrival, and in the evening met together. Mr. O'C——

13

was not in the habit of drinking, but this evening he was led on until he found that he had taken too much.

He rose early the next morning, according to his usual custom, and having heard a great deal of Father Mathew, who was just then beginning to be much talked about (1838), he determined he would "get a look at him" before he went home.

Curiosity was his only motive. He inquired where he could be seen, and was told by the sleepy waiter of the hotel, that Father Mathew always said mass at seven o'clock. Mr. O'C—— set off for Father Mathew's church just to get the one look. He arrived there a little before seven, and seeing that the confessional was occupied, he concluded that the "Apostle was there," and thought he would have time enough just to get one peep at him through the door and be off.

He came as near as he thought he could safely, and tried to take the peep; but to

his great astonishment, he found himself
fairly fixed on the place where he stood, and
not one step could he move one way or the
other.

He was neither fanciful nor superstitious;
such a thing had never happened to him
before, nor to any one else that he had ever
heard of. He knew but little of the lives
of the saints, and was not aware that somewhat similar occurences might be read of in
their histories.

He got very uncomfortable, as well he
might. He could see the people were
looking at him; and at last Father Mathew
came out of his box, and asked would he
go to confession. By no means, it was the
very last thing he had thought of, and, in
fact, he had not been to the sacrament for a
very long time.

Father Mathew, after using some little
persuasion, returned to his box, and Mr.
O'C——, congratulating himself on not only
having seen, but also having spoken to the

famous priest, prepared to leave the church. Again and again he found himself fastened to the spot by an invisible, but an irresistible power. Then he began to think, perhaps he had better go into the confessional, and when he made a move in that direction he found it quite easy.

He told Father Mathew what had happened, and was then easily induced not only to confess, but even to make a general confession of his whole life; and he positively declares that during that confession, Father Mathew told him of many sins which he had forgotten, and which he could only have known supernaturally.

Father Mathew then desired him to go to the altar and he would give him holy communion. But Mr. O'C—— refused. He thought it right to have made a confession, but he said he could not receive his God without further preparation. But the good Shepherd was watching over him, and would not have him sent away; and Father

Mathew came out of his box, and quietly led him by the hand up to the altar.

After mass he took him round to his house to breakfast, treating him as if he had been an old friend. Poor Mr. O'C—— would gladly have escaped the honor, for he was every moment afraid lest Father Mathew would ask him to take the pledge; that he was fully determined he would not do. He had merely been "overtaken" once in his life; that was saying a good deal for a business man of the day; for a man was obliged, according to the miserable custom of the times, to give his men a glass of whiskey every morning before they went to work. No, he certainly would not take the pledge. He was thankful that he had made his confession and received the most holy sacrament, he resolved to be a better Christian from that day forward; but take the pledge—never.

At breakfast Father Mathew talked about everything except the Temperance move-

13*

ment. Mr. O'C—— felt a little more comfortable, but by no means safe.   Father
Mathew had a very unpleasant habit of getting his own way quietly ; and when he was
bent on making a convert, he seldom failed
in his purpose.

At last the fatal moment came.   Mr.
O'C—— rose up to go and Father Mathew
began in his usual winning accents:

"My dear, don't you think you had better
take the pledge?"

"Never, sir!"   .

And Mr. O'C—— made a rush for the
door; but being naturally a very polite
man, he did not exactly like to run out of
the room, though he knew it was the only
safety.

A long argument followed, but Mr. O'C——
was "stiff and steady."

"Well! well! my dear, I won't ask you
to take the pledge; but kneel down, my
dear; kneel down; that won't do you any
harm."

Mr. O'C—— knelt down, still protesting that he would not take the pledge.

Somewhat to his surprise, Father Mathew did not ask him. But he touched his eyes, his mouth, his ears, his face gently and lovingly, and laid his hand, from time to time, on his head, all the while praying most fervently, though Mr. O'C—— could not hear what he said; but he felt, as he said after, as if he had been in Paradise, and he understood that the holy friar was praying to God to keep his five senses from evil.

After a few minutes, Father Mathew spoke: "Now, my dear, I will not ask you to take the pledge, but I will ask you to promise me not to take any kind of intoxicating drink if you can possibly help it; if you wish for it, or see it before you, just avoid taking it, if possible."

This was no pledge, certainly; and Mr. O'C—— made the desired promise with facility, only too well pleased to escape on such easy terms; so he went off to his business, having first received a warm invitation from Father Mathew to come to him whenever he was in Cork.

The day was occupied in arranging his affairs, and the party met at the hotel for dinner, as they had done on the previous evening. The "materials" for punch were placed on the table, as usual; but, no sooner were they placed near Mr. O'C—— than he felt as much horror of whiskey as a mad dog would of water; or, just to use his own expression, "he could as soon have drunk so much ditch water." He could not take the whiskey, and put it away from him with actual disgust.

Of course, his friends laughed at him, joked him, teased him, and asked him had he taken the pledge. He told them everything, and they only laughed the more; but Mr. O'C—— still found himself in the same difficulty. He had so great an aversion to the whiskey, to spirits of any kind, that he could not touch it.

This continued for two years. At the end of that time Father Mathew visited Killarney, and Mr. O'C—— placed himself in the crowd to take the pledge ; not that it was necessary for him now, but he hoped, by giving the example, that many of his workmen would be induced to do the same. Father Mathew recognized him at once. He took his own medal off his neck and put it on Mr. O'C——, saying, "I knew you would take the pledge." Good Mr. O'C—— is still living, and a fine, hale old man. I have this story from himself. He certainly was the subject of a very special Providence, for there can be little doubt that if he had not visited Father Mathew at that time, he would have been tempted to drink again with his friends the following night, and probably would have thus been led on until he became a confirmed drunkard ; then what would have become of his young helpless family ?

We must then remember that when

Father Mathew disclaimed the power of working miracles himself, he only said what any saint would have said, and what any well educated Catholic would have said, that none but the " Supreme Being," as Protestant writers say, " can work a miracle ; " but Father Mathew knew, as well as we do, that God delegates that power when and where He pleases, to His creatures; and though his humility may have made him doubt that this power was delegated to him, yet the fact still remained the same.

The good people of Cork seem to have been aroused by the Glasgow demonstrations, and to have thought that they too, should pay some additional honor to their own priest.

He had fixed Tuesday, the 23d of August, for his return, and the people determined on that day to show that they, at least, were not of the large class of mankind who give no honor to the prophets of their own country.

There were no railways in Cork in those days, and the stage coach conveyed the holy *soggarth aroon* to his home. At the last stage for changing horses, before entering Cork, the multitudes were assembled to meet him, and the Mayor waited in his carriage to convey the illustrious priest to his home.

In the words of an eye-witness, it seemed as though he had been away years instead of days. The road was thronged with carriages, cars, and every mode of conveyance, for those who could ride, and the crowds who walked were past counting.

Every one was looking out eagerly for the first sight of the coach, or listening, if listening were possible, for the first sound. At last, " He comes!" was the cry of the people. Here was the man of their hearts, the *Soggarth* of Ireland ; for, dear as all our *soggarths* are, they would be the first to give him the special title both of praise and affection.

The various societies were all then in full force, with bands and banners floating on the summer breeze. At length the cry was heard, " He is coming, he is coming!" It was no false alarm now; a moment more and he had come. The coach drove up rapidly, and while shout after shout of welcome was heard, the Apostle of Temperance descended from the public conveyance and took the place prepared for him in the Mayor's carriage.

The societies then formed in order and filed past him with flying flags and the bands playing, while still cheer after cheer rent the air. An address was then read of considerable length, which only said, what every one knew, that Father Mathew had done more good in his day and century than any other living man had done or might ever hope to do. The people of Cork also expressed their gratification at the reception he had been given in Glasgow; and there was a curious allusion to the

railways there, "those mightiest achieve-
ments of science and art," from which one
gathers a regretful feeling that they were
not, as yet, familiar to Cork.

In his reply, Father Mathew again spoke
of that divine charity which was the one
motive of all his actions, the foundation
and ruling principle of his holy life. The
people enjoyed themselves, as only the temperate can, for the rest of the day, and in
the morning Father Mathew's house was
surrounded by crowds, who seemed as if it
were a sufficient enjoyment to be even near
the place where he was.

But Father Mathew was not without some
troubles, even in his own family. Of course,
he wished that they should be, above all, and
more than all, models of temperance; but
there are few of us who can obtain the ac-
complishment of *all* our desires in this
world. None of them, thank God, seem to
have been in any way addicted to intemperance, but that was not enough for their fer-

14

vent relative; he wished that they, at least, should be total abstainers.

And so he believed they were, until he was suddenly aroused from his pleasant dream. It was his custom to pay a yearly visit to his family of two or three days, and this was the only holiday he ever allowed himself. His attachment to children was very great, so, as might be expected, his affection was shown in a very practical manner to his little nephews and nieces, who fondly returned the feeling.

He always came laden with good things for them, and his visit was a general holiday. Water was, of course, the only beverage on the table on such occasions; but his brother John had never formally joined the Temperance Society, and was fond of a glass, though not intemperate.

Father Mathew, however, was not aware of this weakness, and he congratulated his brother openly on his appearance, which he naturally attributed to total abstinence.

John said nothing, but it is probable that he thought a good deal, that he was even then meditating where, and when, and how, he could secure the indulgence.

He had to wait until night, and until his brother Theobald had retired; and then, believing himself to be safe, he proceeded to make himself thoroughly comfortable, and to have a brew of his favorite beverage. He was in the very height of enjoyment, and certainly never more surprised in his life than when he heard a step on the stairs, a step he knew well. The step came nearer, and John knew that his fate was sealed. He hid the sugar, he hid the water, and he had just seized the tumbler, which was too hot for him to hold for more than an instant, when the door opened and the Apostle of Temperance appeared.

Poor John expected a fearful scolding, or to be compelled to take the pledge on the spot; but to his great surprise, his brother only laughed heartily, took the book for which he had returned, and left the room quietly. How far poor John enjoyed his carouse, after this incident, is not left on record ; one thing at least is certain, that he was never complimented again on his personal appearance, nor was he ever held up to an admiring audience as a model of successful Temperance.

CHAPTER XI.

Father Mathew converts a poor Protestant to Temperance by caressing his little child — Miserable effects of drunkenness even in this world — Red Denis — The devil's bargain — Denis wants a "darby" — Father Mathew conquers — Denis becomes a firm teetotaller.

NE very beautiful instance is recorded of Father Mathew's power of winning souls for God, which must be mentioned here. A poor Protestant workman had plunged himself in the very lowest state of misery by the disgusting vice of intemperance. There seemed no human hope of his reformation. His unhappy wife was half naked, and more than half starved; she, like too many an honest woman had the misfortune to be tied to a drunken brute. His poor little innocent children had been trained up to vice and hardened in misery.

14*   (161)

Father Mathew came to see him twice, but without effect. He came again a third time, and was only insulted by the wretched creature. But no insult could prejudice the holy man against any unhappy sinner. He turned to leave the room, for he saw that argument or persuasion were useless; and as he passed one of the little children, he took it up tenderly in his arms, as his Divine Master had done, and after kissing it affectionately, he put it on the floor again, and slipped some money into its tiny hand.

The man saw the action, and by God's good grace it was the means of his conversion. A miracle of grace was wrought upon his soul; he flung himself upon his knees, and cried out amid convulsive sobs: "Oh, my God, pardon me! Here is this good man, who has acted more like a father to my children than I have myself; he would feed them, and I have starved them. God forgive me! God in His mercy forgive me."

He then took the pledge, and kept it faithfully ; thus one more family was saved from
days and years of misery; one more wife
and mother was made happy; and the poor
father himself soon learned that what he
had once believed so necessary for his happiness was, in fact, the once curse of his
life.

One of Father Mathew's most famous
converts was called "Red Denis." He obtained his distinctive appellation from the
color of his hair. Red Denis was a faithful
servant, but he had just the "one fault;"
the fault which is the utter ruin, the temporal ruin, or the eternal destruction of so
many noble souls. His master had long
borne with his failing, but there is a limit
to all human patience, and the unfortunate
drunkard had certainly obtained a much
longer grace than he deserved.

At last he was offered the choice of leaving his situation or taking the pledge. But
Denis loved his enemy too well to part with

him ; and the devil, who knew that his prey was in danger, had a ready temptation to try and keep him safe for hell fire.

It was clear that Denis would make some effort to save his soul. Alas! that he should have been driven to it, not by the love of God, but by the fear of temporal loss. Poor Denis! he was terribly afraid of leaving his place with a good master in this world; but it is to be feared that he thought very little, indeed, of the loss of a place near his Lord forever and forever.

He went to Father Mathew to make his bargain, or the devil's bargain ; for the cruel fiend, if he cannot bind a man by ropes of iron, will try to bind him, aye, and will bind him too, safe and sure by the little silken cord of an evil inclination.

He persuaded Denis, and Denis was quite willing to be persuaded, that he could not do without a "drop;" he knew well that if he only persuaded him to take a "drop," now and again, he would easily persuade

him, after a little, to take a quantity, to im-
merse himself once more in the filthy mire
of the most brutal vice of drunkenness.

But Father Mathew knew the tricks of
the devil too well, and knew from long
years of sad experience that TOTAL ABSTI-
NENCE is the only safety for those who are
tempted by the demon Drink. If a man is
tempted to commit suicide, his friends keep
every sharp instrument from him. If they
lock up his razors, and leave him his pocket
knife, they might as well leave him the
razors too.

So Red Denis went off to Father Mathew,
to see what bargain he could make.

" I thank God you are come to me," exclaimed the good priest, " and of your own
free-will too ; a voluntary sacrifice is most
acceptable to the good God. Kneel down,
my dear child," continued Father Mathew
to the giant, who was scratching his red poll
in great perplexity.

" Well, sir, the truth of it is, you must
make a bargain with me," said Denis.

"Bargain, my dear; what bargain?"

"I'm thinking, your reverence, of giving up the spirits, but"—

"God will bless you, my dear, for doing
so. It never did any one good, and it has
ruined thousands and thousands of immortal souls, too."

"What you say, your reverence, is true
enough; and I'm going to give it up, but I
must have a darby."

"A darby, my dear!"

"Yes, your reverence, one darby a day.
I'll take the pledge if your reverence will
only give me one darby a day."

But Father Mathew would not allow the
"darby." Denis must either take the pledge
altogether or not take it at all, and Denis
declared at last that it was not in the power
of God Almighty to make him do without
the whiskey altogether.

Poor Denis! many and many a man has
thought the same. Many and many a man
has gone from a life of temporal misery in

this world, and to a life of eternal misery in
the next, because he would not believe that
God would help him to overcome his besetting sin. As if God had ever refused his
grace to any one who had asked for it truly
and sincerely. It is, indeed, a favorite trick
of the devil's to try to persuade people that
they cannot resist temptation, and woe to
those who are deceived by his lies. He
would not ask anything better, for it secures
his victims.

Father Mathew desired Denis to come
back in a week, and so he did, happily for
himself. He still held out for the "darby,"
but Father Mathew held out for the grace
of God, and happily for the poor man's soul,
he conquered.

"Kneel down this moment," he said, ad-
dressing his refractory disciple, "and repeat
the words of the pledge after me ; and I tell
you that God *will* give you strength to
resist temptations for the future. I promise
you that He will give you strength and

grace to do so.   I promise it to you in his name."

The good priest's commands were all-powerful.   Denis took the pledge, and not only did he keep it faithfully, but he even declared, again and again, that a "darby would choke him" if he ever attempted to take it.

CHAPTER XII.

 PUBLIC meeting was held in the year 1843, on the 26th of January, in the Theatre Royal, Dublin, to offer some testimonial or public expression of gratitude to Father Mathew for his services to Ireland. The requisition convening 'the meeting was signed by two dukes, four marquises, nineteen earls, ten viscounts and barons, four Catholic bishops, more than forty baronets, and an immense number of clergymen and gentlemen of all religious denominations.

15   (169)

The chair was taken by the Duke of Leinster, who, it will be remembered, had insisted on entertaining Father Mathew when he visited Maynooth.

A letter was read from a celebrated medical man, Dr. Carmichael ; and surely, if there were no other testimony than this, to the blessed effects of Temperance, it should be sufficient to warn those who are straying into, or continuing in a career which, sooner or later, *must* end in the most terrible misery ; which, even while it is indulged in, is so far from promoting the happiness of its victims.

The doctor writes thus:

"RUTLAND SQUARE, Jan. 22d, 1843.

"MY DEAR SIR : I send you a brief memorandum of the facts I accidentally mentioned to you the other day, respecting the cases of admission into the Richmond Surgical Hospital, before Father Mathew's happy influence converted the poor of this city from drunkenness to sobriety.

" The hospital contains 130 beds, chiefly appropriated to surgical cases; and, before the pledge was so generally taken by the poor of the city, we were never without cases of wounds, and broken heads and arms of women, the cruel inflictions of their drunken husbands; when, at the same time, it usually contained cases of infants and children half burned or scalded to death, through the negligence of their drunken mothers. The hospital, I may safely say, was never without cases of delirium tremens, many of which ended fatally. Indeed, I know of no instance of any individual affected with this malady, arising from the abuse of ardent spirits, that did not ultimately die of the disease.

" Now, if we contrast these facts with the records of the hospital since Father Mathew has made us a sober people, we do not find a single instance of wounds, burns, or

scalds, attributable to drunkenness, and seldom or ever is any case of delirium tremens
admitted into the hospital.

"The records of the hospital also prove
that since the great mass of the population
of this city have become sober, the rate of
mortality amongst all descriptions of patients
is considerably reduced ; a proof of the increased strength and power of the lower
orders, in effectually resisting the influence
of the diseases, etc.

"My dear Sir, truly yours,
"RICHARD CARMICHAEL."

"The Marquis of Headford, and the Marquis of Clanricarde, both addressed the
meeting, and Mr. Smith O'Brien added his
testimony.

But there was one speaker who was
listened to with more than ordinary interest, both by those who loved him because
he loved old Ireland, and by those who, we
must fear, hated him for the self-same reason.

Those who would not have ventured to go and hear O'Connell when he spoke for political purposes, were glad of the opportunity of hearing him now, when they could do so without infringing their dignity, while a word from the "Liberator" was enough to gladden the hearts of thousands who had less dignity and more patriotism.

Even while proclaiming the praises of the "Apostle," he still defended Ireland. "It was true," he said—"it could not indeed be denied, that the Irish Nation had been given to the curse of drink; but he denied that they were worse than their neighbors; for he assured the meeting that he had obtained parliamentary statistics which showed that before the Temperance movement, the Scotch drank more than twice as much as the Irish." He concluded by saying, "There is no 'painting the rainbow,' the ray that comes from the sun, or the angelic plumes that flutter round the Diety; and there is no angel more pure or worthy than the

15*

angel of public morality, dignified in the person of Father Mathew."

During the following month, Father Mathew was entertained at a " monster" tea-party in the Corn Exchange at Cork. At this meeting, 1,700 persons were present. When the secretaries came to make up their accounts, they found themselves just one hundred pounds short, and this sum Father Mathew insisted on paying himself.

There can be no doubt whatever, that such gatherings were of the greatest value to the noble and sacred cause to which he had dedicated his life. Money was of no importance to him, except in so far as it could assist that cause ; hence whether it was spent on bands, or tea-parties, or processions, or medals for those who could not afford to purchase them, it was all the same, the end was the greater glory of God; and if that end was to be purchased at the cost of much suffering to the holy friar, he loved it none the less.

Father Mathew's two brothers, Frank and Tom, died in 1843, and he mourned for them long and tenderly. Probably he was saved from extreme depression by his great devotion to his work, for he seems to have had a more than ordinarily sensitive disposition, and family trials weighed on him more heavily than on others.

Ever since the year 1840, he had been urgently pressed to visit England. This visit was now accomplished, and, no doubt, was of very great service to him in distracting his thoughts from the subject of his grief.

Lord Stanhope wrote to him in January, and said he hoped nothing would occur to prevent the visit which was fixed for May, and that it would be hailed with extreme and heartfelt satisfaction by the friends of Temperance, and would be of infinite importance to the cause.

The Apostle visited all the large towns in England, where he administered the pledge to thousands. The Catholic clergy received him with the greatest warmth; which, indeed, they might well do, if only for his nationality, since the greater number of them, then, as now, were Irish. The bishops, also, were anxious that he should be their guest; but he generally refused their hospitality, as he preferred a hotel, where, as he himself said, "he could be free to see all persons, rich and poor, at all hours."

This determination led to an amusing expedient on the part of a good member of the Society of Friends. He had heard of Father Mathew's determination to remain at a hotel, and he knew, every one knew, that when the good Father said a thing, he meant it. But the Friend was positively determined to entertain Father Mathew, so he got a large board and had the word HOTEL painted on it, in large letters, and put up over his door.

Then he waited on Father Mathew and asked him to stop at his hotel, a request to

which he at once acceded. The friend was
greatly pleased. Father Mathew certainly
thought the establishment a model one.
Everything was so orderly ; everything so
quiet ; there was so little bell-ringing ; and
then, all his possible wants were anticipated,
and his few requests attended to with a
promptness which he had certainly never
before experienced in any public establishment.

But Father Mathew was too much occupied in his work, and too innocent himself
ever to suspect any fraud on the part of
others. It was not until he had remained
some days in the " Hotel," that he discovered the trick that had been played
upon him. It was then too late for him to
make any change, even if it had been
necessary..

But his visit to England, however useful
to others, was very trying to himself personally, for he was continually invited to
the houses of great people. These invita-

tions he did not like to decline, because he hoped these great people might be of service to the cause he had at heart; for the rich and noble have often to be won and caressed into doing good works, which seem almost a matter of course to the poor.

If he refused these invitations they would be offended, and, perhaps, would cease to patronize the cause which they ought to have considered it the highest honor to assist. He, like a true Apostle, was obliged to be all things to all men; but in so doing he was obliged to suffer, as all who work earnestly for God must do. The late hours, the disarrangement of his usual habits, the waste of time, or, at least, the loss of time which he was obliged to give to these people, and which he was obliged, also, to take from the few hours which he allowed himself for rest; all this was, indeed, hard to poor human nature; but we cannot doubt that he has his reward for the sacrifice now.

Besides this his life was more than once endangered by the wickedness of those who thought that by killing him, they could do themselves service, for they would not ever make a pretence that it was for God.

It is to the everlasting credit of the Irish Protestants, as well as Catholics, that they never offered any serious opposition, and were very far from offering anything even approaching to violence, to the man who certainly injured the trade of great numbers. But it was not so in England. The public-house keepers at Bermondsey and Westminster attacked the Apostle violently, and only for the Irish, who were too numerous in those parts of London to be treated with impunity, it is almost certain that Father Mathew would have fallen a victim to their violence.

Even the English Protestant papers admitted this, though they did not make any observations on the difference between Saxon and Celtic morality. An attempt was

even made to break down the platforms occupied by Father Mathew and his friends,
which, if it had succeeded, would have
caused a most fearful sacrifice of human
life. How terrible is the infatuation, how
cruel the policy of those who are willing to
destroy hundreds for their own selfish ends!
And yet, terrible as this seems, it was only
the life of their body which could have
been injured by this diabolical scheme. Are
there not hundreds who deliberately destroy, or, at least, assist in the destruction
of their fellow-creatures, by tempting them,
by actually advising them to take intoxicating drinks, which are poison to their
souls?

Protestant prejudice was also worked on,
as it has been worked on again and again?
both in England and America, for wicked
ends.

When nothing else would keep the people
from the holy friar, the cry was raised that
he was a " papist," and that no good Protest-

ant should go near him, or get his blessing; as if Protestants had not souls to save as well as Catholics; as if they were not in as much, and even more danger, from the demon Drink.

Truly, it matters little to the Devil how he hinders a good work, so long as it is hindered.

But if the holy priest was tried by the enemy, he was, also, a little consoled by the faithful. The noble family of the Duke of Norfolk have always been forward in every good work. The name of Norfolk has been, and still is, seen in all lists of charitable subscriptions, and the munificence of each member of the family is only exceeded by their piety.

It was, then, a special source of joy and consolation to Father Mathew, when he saw the head of that noble house on his knees before him, asking for the pledge, like the poorest Irishman. For once, he hesitated to give it. He knew the value of such an

16

accession to the ranks of Temperance, but
he knew also, that gentlemen in the position
of this nobleman might find extreme difficulty
in practising total abstinence, even though
they might be most anxious to do so; he
feared, also, that some impulse of enthusiasm
might be the cause of so unusual an action.

But, the noble youth assured him that he
had received Holy Communion that morning, and that he had reflected carefully on
the step which he was about to take.   This
was sufficient, and the illustrious name was
at once added to the roll of honor.

Father Mathew had an interview with the
Duke of Wellington about the same time.
Father Mathew claimed the Duke as a
disciple.

"How can that be, Father Mathew?" he
replied. "I am not a teetotaller; though I am
a very moderate man."

"Oh, but you are a temperate man, your
grace," he answered; "for if you had not so

cool a head, you would not have been the illustrious Duke of Wellington. .

And this certainly was true; for no man given to intemperance, has ever distinguished himself in any art or profession.

CHAPTER XIII.

HE Protestant bishop of Norwich, Dr. Stanley, a very celebrated man, was one of the many gentlemen who were anxious to show respect and hospitality to Father Mathew. He arranged for a meeting to honor the Apostle and his cause, and also requested the favor of his company at his own house, at any time or hour that might be most convenient.

Father Mathew accepted the invitation, and his visit to Norwich was not one of the least successful or remarkable of his many triumphs in England.

(184)

He had a very busy time of it after his return back again to Cork; for all his work was in arrear, and the very fame of all he had done in England, helped to bring many a poor fellow to his feet; besides this, he was necessarily occupied with visitors, each of whom thought he had a good claim on Father Mathew's time and attention.

Visitors came from England, from Scotland, from the Continent of Europe, and from America, and all were received with equal courtesy and attention, and treated as if the good friar's only object in life was receiving company, and hospitality. On such occasions a sudden interruption would occur to the conversation, no matter what the subject might be.

Father Mathew's heart was in his work; and while he played the host to the delight and admiration of his visitors, he still managed to " keep an eye " on the window ; for from the window he could see any stray sheep who might be coming to him,

16*

half in hope, and half in fear. He knew well how hard the struggle was, how busy the demon was, how the cruel wolf was watching to see would it not be possible to spring on his prey, even at the last moment. Indeed, the last moment was what seemed to be most dangerous, for the last effort of diabolical malice and craft would be made then.

And so the true Father, the good shepherd, was ready for the foe, and with one spring he would dart from his seat and run out to welcome the poor sinner, and lead him in with triumph and love. It mattered little to him who the visitor might be, the poor soul's salvation was of far more consequence. When his mission was accomplished, he would return and resume the conversation until another call came for the exercise of his sublime charity.

His correspondence was of necessity very large, and some of the letters he received were curious productions. There were some who had taken the pledge in a sort of enthusiasm, and of these were some who wanted to be released from its restraints. They did not like to break their vow deliberately, and so they wanted a release from "his reverence," trying to save their consiences by this artifice, and yet to indulge their unhappy propensities. An immediate reply was always and urgently demanded by these poor people, they, like many others, fancying that their affairs were of the greatest moment, and not being able to understand that his "reverence" had many other occupations besides attending to their little requests.

Many and many an hour the poor Father was obliged to steal from his rest, which seemed absolutely necessary in order to attend to the countless claims on his time and patience ; but he never murmured.

His servant, John, who was a character, and certainly the master's master, was the cause in various ways of many trials. Sometimes when Father Mathew managed to get a short time early in the day for letter-writing, he was visited by his domestic, who, for what reason it is impossible to say, took this special opportunity for trying his patience.

He would make dusting an excuse for conversation, and after much unnecessary cleaning of articles already clean, he would at last make a raid on Father Mathew's desk. This was really too much even for the patience of the Apostle; and he would at last exclaim, " John, if you continue to go on in this dreadful way, I declare I must leave the house."

But Father Mathew's greatest trial now, and probably the very greatest trial of his whole life, was the pecuniary difficulties in which he became involved in consequence of his immense charity. The noblemen and gentlemen who were so anxious to pay him honor in England and Ireland, never seem to have thought it at all necessary to give him any pecuniary assistance in his work.

They talked a great deal; it was, certainly, very pleasant to honor themselves by honoring this good man; but there the matter ended; the talk certainly cost nothing, and it gave them a little temporary fame.

This was very pleasant, very unexpensive, and very worthless.

The evil was also very much aggravated by the fact, that it was generally supposed that Father Mathew was wealthy : every one supposed that every one else gave him money; it was a convenient excuse for personal parsimony ; and, then, it was said, that he must have made thousands, nay, more, millions of money by the sale of his temperance medal.

Poor Father Mathew ! and, yet, we may not dare to call him poor ; for, perhaps, the trials he endured in this matter, though, or rather because they almost broke his heart, are now the brightest jewels of his eternal crown. There are few saints, indeed, who have not been calummniated and tried in some way or other, who have not had to suffer from the lying misrepresentations of enemies, or the ignorance of friends, and our holy Irish *soggarth* was not an exception to this general rule.

His medals, by which he had been supposed to make so much money, were an actual source of loss to him, and heavy loss too. He gave the medals away by thousands; and this was absolutely necessary. It was the very poorest who came to him for the pledge; it was the very poorest who needed to take it most; and at that very time, it was stated on official authority, that there were two millions and a half of people in Ireland who were all but utterly destitute.

At last Father Mathew was arrested in Dublin by a bailiff, while administering the pledge; this aroused his friends, and he was

obliged to allow Mr. Maguire, now M. P. for
Cork, a man who has never ceased working
for God and Ireland, to assist in some way
in obtaining the necessary means for free-
ing himself from debt, and for carrying on
his great work.

His friends did not fail him, and he was
released from embarrassment, but only for
the time. The great "demonstrations"
which had been held in Dublin sometime
before, at which so many people talked so
much, and did so little, turned out useless
for all practical purposes, as such demonstrations generally do. The great people
who made speeches never gave one penny
to the object of the meeting, and the "expenses" were not nearly covered by the
receipts, so that there was actually a debt
left after the affair was concluded.

Of the famine year, with all its horrors, we
are happily not obliged to write at present.
It must, however, be observed, that Father
Mathew devoted himself then to his people,

with greater assiduity and self-sacrifice than
ever, if that were.possible.

He cared both for their bodies and their
souls; he strove unceasingly to obtain sup-
plies of food from the wealthy English people, to whom his name alone was a sufficient recommendation; and he proclaimed the
necessity of Temperance more and more, as
well he might. The vice of drunkenness,
terrible and degrading as it is at all times,
was then, if possible, still more terrible and
still more degrading.

"I am here," he said, "on one occasion,
in the name of the Lord. I am here for your
good. This is a time to try men's souls;
and that man or that woman must be a
·monster who would drink while a fellow-
creature was dying for want of food. I
don't blame the brewers or the distillers; I
blame those who make them so. If they
could make more money in any other way,
they would; but, while so many of the
people are fools enough to buy and drink

their vile manufactures, they will continue in the trade. Is it not a terrible thing to think that so much wholesome grain, that God intended for the support of human life, should be converted into a maddening poison, for the destruction of human bodies and souls?"

17

CHAPTER XIV.

HE people of America had rendered
great assistance to Ireland in the
famine year. On the 13th of April,
1847, the Jamestown arrived in Cork, laden
with provisions, and commanded by Captain
Forbes, who was the bearer of an invitation
to Father Mathew. Captain Forbes was
most anxious to take Father Mathew back
with him to America, but the true-hearted
soggarth would not leave his country in her
hour of need. The commander of another

vessel also came to him before leaving Cork, to try and persuade Father Mathew to make the return voyage with him; but he would not leave his post.

Dr. Murphy, the Catholic bishop of Cork, died on the 7th of April, 1847; and the clergy of Cork unanimously elected Father Mathew as his successor. The good priest could not but feel gratified at such a cordial evidence of their confidence in him, and of their respect for him ; and as he believed that his elevation to the Episcopate would contribute to the advancement of his work, he was both ready and willing to accept the dignity.

But this dignity was not to be his. The holy see decided against the votes of the clergy, and the present bishop of Cork, the Right Rev. Dr. Delany, was elevated to the Episcopal bench. There is no doubt that this decision was a wise one, and that a bishop needs very special qualifications, which qualifications Father Mathew, with all his zeal and sincerity, had not.

His work was in another sphere; his ca-
pabilities of usefulness of another order.
The cares of a diocese, if properly attended
to, would be sufficient for any one man;
but, if he had attempted to combine with
those cares the labors of his Apostolic life, he
must have failed in both.

In the year 1847, the English government
performed one of its few acts of justice to
Ireland, by allowing Father Mathew an
annual pension of three hundred pounds.
But he was none the richer for it. He
never expended a penny on himself that
was not of absolute necessity, and this
money was now devoted to paying the
policy of an insurance on his life for the
sole benefit of his creditors.

Father Mathew had always observed the
fasts of the church with great strictness;
but neither his advancing years, nor his
many labors, labors which might well have
broken down the strongest man, were allowed by him as a plea for the very least

dispensation. When expostulated with by any of his friends on this subject, he would say "that he was the strongest man in Ireland," and turn off the conversation with a pleasant smile.

He fasted with his usual strictness, and worked with his usual zeal during the heat of 1848; but one morning, when trying to rise from bed at his usual early hour, he fell prostrate on the ground, struck down by paralysis.

His secretary, who slept in the room below, heard the fall, and ran to his assistance. He was helped back to bed, and the doctor sent for—an old friend. On his arrival, Father Mathew told him, with one of his sweetest smiles, and as if it were not a matter of the least consequence, that he had been struck with paralysis.

While the usual remedies were being applied, he talked calmly to his friends, and said, "it was not much matter how it ended. If a priest had done his duty, and was pre-

17*

pared, the time of his death was of little consequence." And in truth, for him, the sooner he died, the sooner he would obtain his crown, and enter the rest he had earned by his life of labor; but for poor Ireland it was necessary that he should live a little longer, that he should suffer and work a little more; and the cries of her faithful children ascended before the throne of God, and were heard by Him. In a few weeks the Apostle of Temperance was so far recovered as to be able to resume his labors for them once more.

After his recovery he visited Dublin, where he gave evidence for Mr. Gavin Duffy, at the State Trials, and continued his usual occupation of administering the pledge. In 1849, he carried out his long-planned idea of visiting America. His friends and his physicians tried to dissuade him from this undertaking on account of his recent illness; but it is probable that the very reason which they adduced for preventing him from undertaking it, was the very reason which induced him to undertake it.

They feared that his health, already undermined by paralysis, would suffer severely from such an attempt, and that his valuable life would be shortened. He knew full well that one attack of paralysis was the sure precursor of another, that the hour might come soon when he could no longer work, and that his work should be accomplished if possible before that hour.

The night was coming, that night which must precede the dawn. Like all the saints he felt that there would be time enough for rest in Heaven. Like all the saints, he wished to devote every moment of his time to his Master's service.

He knew that he might never see his family or friends again, and he bid them all an affectionate farewell before setting out. A voyage to America then was by no means the quick and easy passage that it is to-day, and Father Mathew suffered much from the

confinement which proved so great a contrast to his ordinary mode of life. Still he
was not idle. How could he be? And as
soon as he recovered from the usual sick-
ness of the first few days, he devoted himself to the emigrants who were on board,
and spent the greater part of his time with
them, hearing their confessions, administering the pledge, or giving them good advice.

On his arrival in New York, he was received by Mr. Nesmith who took him at
once to his own house, where he rested until the next day, when he was to receive a
public reception. The "rest" was certainly a short one, but it was long enough for
his zeal.

On Monday, 2d July, 1849, Father
Mathew was welcomed to America by the
municipal authorities, Alderman Hawes
taking the lead. He proceeded in the
steamer Sylph to Staten Island, the Castle
Garden having been chosen as the place of

meeting. The whole city turned out in holiday array, and the cheers of the faithful Irish, though not as numerous a body then as now, were heard in every quarter. May- or Woodhull invited him to accept the hos- pitalities of the city, and well had it pre- pared for the reception of the illustrious guest.

The " Herald" thus describes the reception at the Irving House :

" As you enter the hall, a life-like painting of Father Mathew meets your eye, at the further end right over the bar ; and in the lobby window, immediately behind, and a little above, there is a beautiful white satin blind, with the inscription " Glory be to God on high ; and on earth peace to men of good will ;" then immediately underneath, the word " Temperance !" At the front of this is an exquisitely painted wreath of flowers, with Father Mathew's autograph, in large hand in the centre. The suite of rooms are on the second floor, and consist of four, a reception-parlor, a drawing-room, and a bed-room, all on the same range, and com- · municating with each other, and a dining-room at the other side of the hall.

"These rooms are all furnished with the newest and richest furniture, and in the most modern style of fashion. The tables, chairs and sofas of the finest massive rosewood; the carpets, tapestry, velvets, and every thing else in keeping. The bedstead is also of rosewood and has a magnificent lace canopy."

Father Mathew was entertained at a public banquet, in the evening, where he drank the health of the Mayor and citizens of New York in a bumper of water. Probably a sincerer toast was never proposed or quaffed. At last he was persuaded to return for the night, but he managed to avoid the lace-curtained couch which had been prepared for him, and took his rest in an humble bed which had been assigned to his secretary.

For a fortnight he held levees in the City Hall, to which rich and poor, high and low, young and old, thronged by thousands. It was indeed a scene which had never before been witnessed in any great city; such as probably will never be witnessed again. All classes of men came to him and he received them alike, for it was souls he sought. The soul of the peasant was as dear to him, and it was also to his Master, as the soul of the man who counted his dollars by millions.

His affectionate heart was not a little touched by the love which the poorer classes showed him. The *soggarth* from old Erin would have been welcome to them, even if he had not been Father Mathew. Father Mathew with his usual thoughtful charity generally inquired from what part of Ireland each visitor came; and he generally had some news to tell them, in return, of that part of the dear old land they loved so well.

The fatigue of these visits must have

been immense, but, as he had said himself,
" what matter?" It is only when people work
very hard for God that their friends get
anxious, lest they should break down or
overwork themselves ; when they are laboring for temporal affairs, no one concerns
himself; and yet if a man is praised for working hard to place his family well in this
world, how much more should a man be
praised for working hard to raise hundreds
and thousands of souls to the very highest
place in the kingdom of heaven.

Father Mathew's next visit was to Bos-
ton, where an attempt was made to try and
induce him to join one public party in pref-
erence to another, a proceeding which
would have been highly injurious to his
work. With consummate prudence Father
Mathew avoided the trap which was set for
him, and declared that the Temperance cause
was his one object, and that he could not
identify himself with any other, no matter
what that other might be.

The result was a stormy controversy, in which Father Mathew was blamed by both sides, and sometimes in very bitter language. It was certainly a pitiful exhibition of human nature. Had he taken a side, the rejected party might have had some excuse for annoyance; but, his neutrality ought to have protected him, even if his mission had not done so. His sensitive and delicate mind suffered from all this in a way which his persecutors, we must hope, could never have understood; and this, with incessant labor, brought on a severe illness in the fall. He recovered, however, and visited Washington in December, when a resolution was unanimously carried in Congress, admitting him to a seat on the floor of the House. When he availed himself of this compliment, the members rose in a body to receive him.

A proposal to offer him a similar honor was made in the Senate, but the stupid prejudices of some individual produced an

18

opposition ; the resolution, however, was
passed by a considerable majority ; and on
Thursday, the 20th December, 1844, Father
Mathew was entertained by the President
of the United States, at a banquet, to
which fifty of the leading men of the day
were invited. Though wine was placed on
the table, the host and many of the party refrained from the indulgence, out of respect
to their guest.

CHAPTER XV.

ATHER MATHEW was again attacked by paralysis while going up the Mississippi from New Orleans to Nashville. He had already begun to feel home-sick, and had written to that effect to his devoted friend, Mrs. Rashbourne, the wife of a merchant prince in Liverpool famous for his charities. The following extract from an address which he delivered in Cincinnati a few months before this attack, will show what he felt and suffered:

" In the protracted warfare which I have

waged against the wide-spread evil of intemperance, and which, I trust, has ever
been conducted in a spirit of Christian
charity, I have had many serious difficulties
to encounter, and much interested hostility
to overcome. The growing infirmities of
age, aggravated by repeated attacks of a
dangerous and insidious malady, now de-
mand retirement and repose. At the close
of a long and, thank Heaven, a successful
campaign, I find myself, it is true, enfeebled
in health, shattered in constitution, and
destitute of this world's wealth, yet, with
the Apostle, 'I glory in my infirmity,'
contracted as it has been, in the noblest of
causes; and I still feel that no sacrifice,
whether of health, of property, or of life
itself, is too great, to save from ruin and
perdition, the humblest of those for whom
our Divine Saviour has willingly shed His
most precious blood."

He embarked for Europe on the 8th Nov.,
1851, in the Pacific; but before he left the

American shore he published a "farewell" address to the citizens of the United States, which commences thus:

"My mission amongst you closes to-day. I cannot take my final departure from the shores of your great and generous country without publicly recording my deep and grateful appreciation of the generous sympathy, the delicate attention, and the unremitting kindness which I have experienced in every section of this vast Union. The noble reception which you have spontaneously tendered to a stranger, known merely as an humble missionary in the cause of Temperance reform, proves the devotion of your people to the interests of humanity, however feebly championed, and has endeared America and her people to me by a thousand ties too sacred for utterance.

"Though the renewed attacks of a painful and insidious malady have rendered it impossible that I could (without imminent danger to my life) make those public ex-

18*

ertions which were never spared by me, in the days of my health and of my vigor, I thank heaven I have been yet instrumental in adding to the ranks of Temperance over 600,000 disciples in America. I have been much cheered during the past week by the receipt of letters from all parts of the States, bearing unimpeachable testimony to the strict fidelity with which this voluntary obligation is observed. I need scarcely add, that virtue and the duties which religion inculcates, together with peace, plenty, domestic comfort, health and happiness, have everywhere followed in its train."

The " New York Herald" wrote thus of his mission :

" On reviewing his exertions for the past two years and a half, we are forcibly struck with the vast amount of physical fatigue which he must have undergone in the discharge of his onerous duties. Over sixty years of age, enfeebled in health, and

shattered in constitution, he has yet, with
all the ardor of his former zeal, vigorous-
ly prosecuted his labor of love. He has
visited since his arrival in America twenty-
five States of the Union, has administered
the Temperance pledge in over three hundred of our principal towns and cities, has
added more than half a million of our population to the long muster-roll of his disciples, and, in accomplishing this praiseworthy
object, has travelled thirty-seven thousand
miles, which, added to two voyages across
the Atlantic, would make a total distance
nearly equal to twice the circumnavigation
of the globe. Though laboring under a
disease which the slightest undue excite-
ment may render fatal, never has he shrunk
from his work of benevolence and love.
North and south, east and west, was he to
be seen unostentatiously pursuing the
heavenly task of reclaiming his fallen brother,
welcoming the prodigal son back into the
bosom of society, uttering the joyful tidings

that no man is past the hour of amendment, dealing in no denunciation, indulging in no hypocritical cant or pretensions to exceptional sanctity, but quietly and unobtrusively pursuing his peaceful course, and, like his illustrious sainted prototype, reasoning of ' temperance, justice and judgment to come.' When his physicians recently recommended absolute repose, in the midst of his labors in a crowded town, as indispensable to his recovery from the last attack of paralysis, ' Never,' said the venerable man, ' will I willingly sink into a state of inglorious inactivity, never will I desert my post in the midst of -the battle.' ' But your life,' replied his physician, ' is at stake.' ' If so,' said he, ' it cannot be sacrificed in a better cause. If I am to die, I will die in harness.' "

After his return to Ireland, Father Mathew went to reside. at Lehenagh with his own family, where it was hoped he might recover his health. Here he had

another fit, but this was apoplexy. He was
so little aware of it, however, that when he
awoke in the morning, he said to his faithful attendant, " David, this is the Feast of
the Purification, I must prepare to say Mass."
His devotion to the adorable sacrifice was
indeed very great, and he never omitted
celebrating it every day, no matter how
great might have been the fatigue of the day
preceding. About ten months before his
death, he staggered one day immediately after the Consecration at Mass, and nearly fell.
The clerk came quietly to his assistance, and
he continued the adorable sacrifice, but he
never again ventured to celebrate it.

He was now taken to Madeira, where he
remained some months, but he rallied only for
a little. His time had come. May we all be
as ready for the summons, when we shall be
called. After his return to Ireland, he removed to Queenstown, where he might have
been seen, day after day, tottering along in
some sunny spot, with his hand on the

shoulder of a boy who attended him. It was a pitiful sight, and one which could not be witnessed without deep emotion.

This man, once so full of strength, even as he himself said, probably the strongest man in Ireland, could not now walk alone. Perhaps it was necessary for his perfect sanctification that he should endure this last humiliation, for such it was to him. Perhaps as he had not even known weakness for so many years of his life, it was necessary that he should know it even now.

He was still the same tender, loving, affectionate Father; still the same true-hearted friend, and he had still the great cause as the one object of his life.

At last the summons came. He had spent most of his time in prayer for months. Often when his friends came in to see him, they found him on his knees; and when they spoke of his well-spent life, of all the good he had done, he would beg of them, with touching humility, to change the subject.

A few days before his death he received the last and fatal attack of paralysis. He lay for several days, conscious, but scarcely able to articulate. Even then he made signs that some persons who wished to take the pledge from him should be allowed into his room, and he lifted his palsied hand to make on them the holy sign.

He passed away calmly and peacefully, as one in sleep, on the Feast of the Immaculate Conception, December the 8th, 1856. Can we doubt that Mary came for her faithful son, and took him herself to his eternal reward.

Of his funeral we must not speak. He lies in the cemetery he himself planned, and in the place he himself chose, under the shadow of the Cross. Here the poor come to pray, and here they obtained, through his intercession, such blessings as are only heard of as having been obtained through the merits and intercessions of the saints.

The Protestant patriot, Smith O'Brien,

even thus writes of him: "For myself,
whether he be or be not canonized as a saint
of the Church of Rome, I am disposed to
regard him as an Apostle who was specially
deputed on a divine mission by the Almighty, and invested with power almost
miraculous. To none of the ordinary op-
erations of human agency can I ascribe
the success which attended his efforts to
repress one of the besetting sins of the Irish
nation. If I had read in history that such
success had attended the labors of an un-
pretending priest, whose chief characteristic
was modest simplicity of demeanor, I own
that I should have distrusted the narrative
as an exaggeration; but we have been all
of us witnesses to the fact that myriads
simultaneously obeyed his advice, and, at
his bidding, abandoned a favorite indulgence."

He is dead, indeed, as far as this world is
concerned, or, perhaps, we should rather
say, as far as his temporal mission with this

world is concerned. But he still lives. He lives in the memory of millions of his fellow-countrymen. He lives in the work which he began, and which we may hope will be perpetuated in his name, and assisted by his intercession, as long as the demon Drink needs to be exorcised from the bodies of men.

He lives; let it be ours to honor him, to honor the noblest of Irishmen even now, by our faithful co-operation in his work; and let us be assured that if the angels of heaven know of and rejoice over the repentance of one sinner, so, also, do the saints know and rejoice, when we imitate their example, when we invoke their assistance, when we honor them by our fidelity to their teaching.

Let us ask ourselves, When our time comes to die, as come it must, shall we desire to have a holy, peaceful end like his, or do we desire to be the prey of devils?

As we live, so shall we die. We can now make our choice. If nothing else can give

19

us courage to resist the demon of Intemperance, if he is hunting us on to our ruin, let us think of death, and ask ourselves how we shall answer to God at that dreadful hour, if we willfully cast from us the means of our salvation, if we have refused the assistance offered to us in the sacraments and by Temperance Societies, to overcome our evil inclinations.

A drunken Irishman is a disgrace to Ireland and to religion. A sober Irishman has never yet failed to keep his place with honor, whatever may be his state in life.

THE END.

Let us say the prayer, " Sweet Heart of Mary, be my Salvation" (300 days' indulgence), and " My Jesus Mercy," 100 days' indulgence, for the promotion of Temperance Societies.